Leslie and Mary Jean
Woodley and Betty Hudson

BOARDING HOUSE REACH

Ate supper
here. Food not too
good % (Smith House)

Compiled by
Dot Gibson

First Printing, 1982 - 10,000 copies
Second Printing, 1983 - 10,000 copies
Third Printing, 1986 - 10,000 copies

ISBN-0-941162-001

Copyright© 1981 Dot Gibson Publications
1603 Rainbow Drive
Waycross, Ga. 31501

If you have never enjoyed the unique experience of sitting down to a Smith House table you just simply do not know what you have missed. It is a "seeing is believing" situation. It is like taking a step back in time - to a time of the boarding house and small mountain inn with the large family style dining table.

An average day at the Smith House will see the tables laden with fried chicken, ham, peas, beans, sweet potatoes, slaw, okra, corn, hot biscuits, honey and a delicious cobbler. Or maybe it will be their famous Smith House Rolls, their fantastic Chestnut Souffle, Fried Steak, squash or Banana Fritters. It really doesn't matter - it is all terrific. It is old fashioned down home cookin' and plenty of it.

If you cannot get to Dahlonega, Ga. to experience this meal the next best thing is to use the famous Smith House Cookbook, the BOARDING HOUSE REACH, and prepare those southern specialties at home. Or possibly you have eaten at the Smith House and have for years wondered what "little something extra" made a dish so special.

Now those recipes are available for you, the faithful Smith House diners and you, the would be diners. Any day of the week you can sit down to the table and use your BOARDING HOUSE REACH.

Illustrations by Susan Coleman

Printed in the United States of America
Moran Printing Company
Orlando, Florida

Breads

BREADS

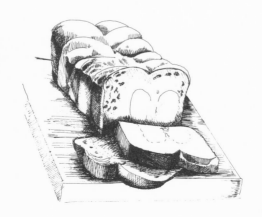

BREADS

SMITH HOUSE ROLLS

1 package yeast
1 1/2 cups lukewarm water
2 eggs [unbeaten]
4 tablespoons sugar

1 teaspoon salt
3/4 cups wesson oil
4 1/2 cups plain flour

Dissolve yeast in lukewarm water. Add other ingredients, adding flour last. Make a soft dough. Knead lightly - set aside in a warm place and let rise until double in bulk. Punch dough down and let rise a second time. Roll out on a floured surface, cut with roll cutter (or biscuit cutter). Dip roll in melted butter and fold over. Let rise again 30 to 35 minutes. Bake at 400 degrees for 10 minutes or until lightly browned.

REFRIGERATOR POTATO ROLLS

1 package yeast
1/2 cup luke warm water
1 cup milk, scalded
1 cup mashed potatoes
2/3 cup shortening

1 teaspoon salt
1/2 cup sugar
2 eggs
6 to 8 cups flour

Mash potatoes, add shortening, sugar, salt and eggs. Cream well. Dissolve yeast in lukewarm water, add to luke warm milk, then add to potato mixture. Add enough flour to make a stiff dough. Toss on a floured surface and knead well. Put in a large greased bowl and let rise until doubled in size. Knead slightly. Rub top with melted butter. Cover tightly and refrigerate until ready to use. About 1 hour before baking shape into rolls, cover and let rise until doubled in size. Bake 15 to 20 minutes at 400 degrees.

BEER ROLLS

4 cups bisquick
1 cup beer

1/2 cup sugar

Combine ingredients and bake in muffin tins 15 to 20 minutes at 400 degrees.

ROLLS

1 cup hot water
6 tablespoons shortening
1/4 cup sugar
1 teaspoon salt

1 egg, well beaten
1 package yeast
2 tablespoons warm water
2 1/2 to 3 1/2 cups plain flour

Pour boiling water over shortening, sugar, and salt. Blend and cool. Add egg. Sprinkle yeast on warm water and stir until dissolved. Add to egg mixture. Gradually add flour and blend well. Place in large covered container in refrigerator over night. (Use dough as needed. Will keep for days in refrigerator). When ready to use roll out small amount on floured surface and cut with biscuit cutter. Brush with melted butter, cover and let rise until doubled. Bake 400 degrees for 10 minutes.

QUICK ROLLS

2 cups self-rising flour
1/4 cup mayonnaise

1 to 1 1/2 cups milk

Mix all ingredients together until smooth. Be sure to use mayonnaise - do not substitute. Divide into 12 rolls and place in muffin tins. Bake 400 degrees for 15 minutes.

GARLIC BISCUITS

1 cup flour
1 teaspoon sugar
2 teaspoons cornmeal
2 teaspoons Parmesan cheese
1 teaspoon garlic salt

2 tablespoons shortening
Milk
1 egg white
1 teaspoon water
Sesame seeds

Combine flour, sugar, cornmeal, cheese and garlic salt. Cut in shortening. Add enough milk to make stiff dough. With floured hands, shape into balls, about the size of walnuts. Place in greased muffin pans and turn once to grease both sides. Bake at 325 degrees until lightly brown. Remove and brush with mixture of egg white and water. Sprinkle lightly with garlic salt and sesame seeds. Return to oven until tops are very brown.   Yield: 6 muffins

ANGEL BISCUITS

1 package yeast
2 tablespoons luke warm water
1 teaspoon soda
3 teaspoons baking powder
5 cups flour

4 tablespoons sugar
1 teaspoon salt
1 cup shortening
2 cups buttermilk

Dissolve the yeast in warm water. Combine flour, soda, baking powder, salt, and sugar. Cut in shortening until size of peas. Add buttermilk and then yeast mixture. Stir until flour is dampened. Knead on floured surface. Roll out and cut into biscuits. Bake 8 to 10 minutes in a 400 degree oven. Dough can be stored in tightly covered container in refrigerator for 2 weeks.

SELF-RISING BISCUITS

2 cups self rising flour
5 tablespoons lard

Mixture of 1/2 milk and
1/2 buttermilk

Cut lard into flour, add enough milk mixture to moisten. Roll out dough on floured surface and cut with a biscuit cutter. Bake on an ungreased baking sheet for 12 to 15 minutes at 450 degrees.

SWEET POTATO BISCUITS

2 cups self-rising flour
1/8 teaspoon salt
1/3 cup shortening

1 cup cooked mashed
sweet potatoes
1/3 cup sweet milk

Preheat oven to 400 degrees. Grease cookie sheet. Sprinkle salt on potatoes. Sift flour. Cut shortening and potatoes into flour. Add milk gradually (more or less according to potatoes). Mix well and roll out. Cut with biscuit cutter or shape with hands. Bake on ungreased pan for 12 to 15 minutes in preheated oven. Butter and serve hot.

APPLE MUFFINS

1/2 cup shortening
1 cup sugar
1 teaspoon cinnamon
3/4 cups milk
2 cups flour

2 1/2 teaspoons baking powder
3/4 teaspoon salt
2 eggs
2 apples, peeled and chopped

Cream shortening and sugar. Mix in the rest of the ingredients, adding apples last. Bake in greased muffin pans at 350 degrees for 15 minutes.

BRAN MUFFINS

2 cups bran cereal
1 1/4 cups milk
1/2 cup molasses
1 egg, well beaten

1/2 teaspoon salt
1 cup sifted all purpose flour
1 teaspoon baking soda
1/2 cup raisins

Combine bran, milk, molasses, egg and let stand five minutes. Add sifted dry ingredients and raisins. Mix. Fill medium greased muffin pans about 2/3 full. Bake at 400 degrees about 20 minutes.

BLUEBERRY LEMON MUFFINS

1 3/4 cups all-purpose
1/2 cup sugar
2 1/2 teaspoons baking powder
3/4 teaspoon salt
3/4 cup milk

1/3 cup vegetable oil
1 egg, beaten
1 cup blueberries
1 teaspoon grated lemon rind
2 tablespoons sugar

Mix blueberries and lemon rind with 2 tablespoons of sugar and set aside. Combine flour, 1/2 cup sugar, baking powder, and salt. Beat egg with fork and add milk and oil. Stir into flour mixture. Stir just enough to moisten. (there should be some lumps). Gently fold in blueberries and lemon rind. Fill greased muffin tins 2/3's full. Bake for 25 minutes at 400 degrees.

OATMEAL MUFFINS

1 cup flour
1 cup quick oatmeal
2 teaspoons baking powder
1/2 teaspoon salt

1 egg, beaten
2 tablespoons sugar
1 cup milk
1/4 cup butter, melted

Combine flour, oatmeal, baking powder, salt, and sugar. Mix well. Mix egg, milk, and butter. Add dry ingredients to egg mixture, stirring only until flour mix is moistened. Fill greased muffin pans 2/3's full. Bake at 400 degrees for 20 minutes.

Yield 10 to 12 muffins

SWEET MUFFINS

2 cups plain flour
3 teaspoons baking powder
2 tablespoons sugar
1 teaspoon salt

1 egg
1 cup milk
3 tablespoons oil

Sift flour, baking powder and salt together. Beat egg. Add sugar and oil mixing well. Alternate milk and flour mixture beating well. Pour into lined muffin pans. Bake 20 to 25 minutes at 450 degrees.

CRACKLIN CORN BREAD

1 1/2 cups corn meal
1 teaspoon salt
2 tablespoons flour
3 teaspoons baking powder

1 egg beaten
1 1/4 cups sweet milk
1 1/2 cups cracklings

Sift corn meal, salt, flour and baking powder together. Mix egg and milk and add to dry ingredients. Mix well and add cracklings. Bake in greased pan in 425 degree oven for about 20 to 25 minutes.

SOUR CREAM CORNBREAD

1 cup self-rising cornmeal
2 eggs, beaten
1/2 cup salad oil

1 (8 ounce) can cream
  style corn
1 cup commercial sour cream

Combine cornmeal, oil, slightly beaten eggs, and corn. Fold in sour cream. Pour into a greased 9 inch pan or muffin tins. Bake 20 to 30 minutes at 400 degrees.

HOT PEPPER CORNBREAD

1 1/2 cups yellow corn meal
3 eggs
2/3 cup oil
3 teaspoons baking powder
1 teaspoon sugar
1 (8 ounce) can cream corn

1 cup milk
1 cup sharp grated cheese
3 or 4 hot peppers
5 green onions (tops too)
1/2 bell pepper, chopped
1 small jar pimientos

Combine all the ingredients and mix well. Pour into a 8x11 greased pan. Bake 30 minutes at 425 degrees.

CORNBREAD

1 1/2 cups cornmeal
1/2 cup all purpose flour
1 teaspoon salt
2 tablespoons sugar
3 teaspoons baking powder

1/2 teaspoon soda
1 egg, slightly beaten
1 1/2 cups sour milk or
   buttermilk
2 to 3 tablespoons shortening

Sift dry ingredients together. Add egg, buttermilk and shortening and stir until well blended. Pour into a preheated 10 inch greased square pan. Bake at 425 degrees for 30 minutes.

Yield: 6 to 8 servings

CORN LIGHT BREAD

1 cup scalded milk
6 tablespoon sugar
2 teaspoons salt
1 stick margarine
3 1/2 cups unsifted flour

2 packages dry yeast
1/2 cup warm water
2 beaten eggs
1 3/4 cups corn meal

Into scalded milk melt and dissolve sugar, salt and margarine. Dissolve yeast in warm water. Combine in large bowl the corn meal and flour. Add milk mixture, yeast and eggs. Stir until well blended. Knead on lightly floured board until smooth and easy to handle (a short time only). Cut dough into two parts (if using regular loaf pans), into 4 if using smaller loaf pans. Let dough rise until doubled in size. Bake at 350 degrees for 20 to 25 minutes. When almost done, pour melted margarine or butter over the top for browning. Lovely with ham, beef, hot or cold or just plain with butter and honey.

Yield: 2 loaves

SALT RISING BREAD

2 medium size Irish potatoes
   thinly sliced
3 tablespoons corn meal
1 1/2 teaspoons salt,
   divided
1 tablespoon sugar

1 quart boiling water
1 pint tepid milk
1/2 pint warm water
Flour

About noon of the first day, mix potatoes, cornmeal, 1 teaspoon salt, sugar and boiling water. Leave in a warm place for fermentation. Next morning strain mixture and add 1/2 teaspoon of salt, milk and warm water. Add enough flour to make a stiff dough. Knead until it blisters. Make into two loaves or rolls. Let rise and bake loaves in a 325 degree oven for 1 1/2 hours. Rolls at 400 degrees for 10 to 15 minutes.

FLUFFY FRENCH TOAST

6 eggs
2 cups milk
1/2 cup plain flour
1 1/2 tablespoons sugar

1/4 teaspoon salt
18 sliced day-old French
   bread, 1 inch thick
1 tablespoon butter

Beat eggs, milk, flour, sugar and salt with rotary beater until smooth. Soak bread in batter until saturated. Melt butter in skillet. Transfer each bread slice into skillet; do not over crowd. Cook over medium heat 12 minutes on each side or until brown.

Yield 18 slices

23

BLACK WALNUT APPLE BREAD

1 1/2 cups sifted all purpose
  flour
2 teaspoons baking powder
1/2 teaspoon baking soda
1 teaspoon salt
1 teaspoon cinnamon
1/4 teaspoon nutmeg
1/8 teaspoon allspice
1 cup broken black walnuts

1 1/2 cups crushed ready-to-
  serve wheat cereal flakes
3/4 cup chopped apple
1 egg, slightly beaten
3/4 cup firmly packed
  brown sugar
1 1/2 cups buttermilk
2 tablespoons vegetable oil

Mix sifted flour, baking powder, baking soda, salt and spices. Stir in cereal flakes, walnuts and apple. Combine egg, brown sugar, butter milk and oil and add to dry ingredients. Mix just enough to moisten dry ingredients completely. Do not beat. Turn into well-greased loaf pan 9x5x3. Bake 350 degrees for 1 hour.

NUT BREAD

3 cups pastry flour-sifted
1 cup sugar
3 teaspoons baking powder
1 teaspoon salt
1 cup chopped nuts

1 egg, beaten lightly
1 cup milk
Chopped cherries and
  dates, optional

Sift flour, sugar, salt and baking powder together twice. Mix egg and milk, and add to flour mixture. Fold in nuts (cherries if desired). Turn into a well-buttered loaf pan and let stand 15 minutes. Bake about 45 minutes at 350 degrees.

Yield: 1 loaf

BANANA DATE BREAD

2 sticks margarine, softened
1 cup sugar
2 eggs
2 cups plain flour
1 teaspoon baking soda

1/2 teaspoon salt
3 large bananas
1/2 teaspoon vanilla
1/2 package of dates

Cream margarine and sugar. Add eggs one at a time. Combine flour, baking soda and salt and add to mixture. Mash bananas and add to mixture. Cut dates in half and add with vanilla to batter. Pour into a well greased 10-inch loaf pan. Bake 1 hour at 350 degrees.

BRAN GINGERBREAD

1 3/4 cups all purpose flour
1 teaspoon baking soda
1/2 teaspoon salt
3/4 teaspoon double-acting
   baking powder
1 teaspoon cinnamon
1/4 teaspoon cloves

1 teaspoon ginger
1/2 cup shortening
1 egg
1 cup molasses
1 cup hot water
2 cups bran cereal, flakes

Mix flour with soda, baking powder, salt, and spices. Cream shortening and beat in egg. Add molasses and hot water and blend well. Add flour mixture and beat until smooth. Stir in cereal. Pour into a 9-inch square pan, which has been lined on bottom with paper. Bake at 325 degrees for 45 minutes. Cool in pan 5 minutes. Remove from pan and finish cooling on rack. Serve warm with prepared whipped topping.

DELICIOUS GINGER BREAD

1 cup dark molasses
1/2 cup brown sugar
1/2 cup oil
1/2 teaspoon cinnamon
1/2 teaspoon cloves
1/2 teaspoon nutmeg
1 teaspoon ginger

2 eggs
1 teaspoon baking soda
   dissolved in 1 tablespoon
   water
1 cup boiling water
2 1/2 cups unsifted flour
Sugar

Blend together molasses, brown sugar, oil, cinnamon, cloves, nutmeg, and ginger. Stir in eggs. Add dissolved soda. Sift in flour and beat well. Add boiling water and beat lightly and quickly. Pour into greased skillet. sprinkle top with sugar and bake 30 minutes at 350 degrees.

APPLE-MOLASSES BREAD

1/2 cut butter or margarine
1 cup sugar
3 eggs
2 cups sifted all-purpose
   flour
1 teaspoon baking powder
1/2 teaspoon salt
1/2 teaspoon baking soda

1/2 teaspoon ground cinnamon
1/2 teaspoon ground nutmeg
1/4 cup molasses
1 cup canned applesauce
1 cup chopped raisins or
   dates
1/4 cup chopped walnuts or
   pecans

Beat butter in electric mixer until soft. Gradually add sugar, beating until light and fluffy. Add eggs, one at a time. Sift together flour, baking powder, baking soda, salt, cinnamon and nutmeg. Combine molasses and applesauce. Add flour mixture, alternating with molasses mixture to the sugar mixture, beating well after each addition. Fold in raisins and nuts. Pour batter into a greased and lightly floured 9x5x3 inch loaf pan. Bake for 1 hour and 15 minutes in a 325 degree preheated oven. Let cool 5 minutes in pan. Remove to wire rack to cool completely. Store, wrapped in refrigerator. Excellent with whipped cream cheese. This bread freezes well.

FIFTH AVENUE ROLL

1/4 teaspoon cinnamon
1/4 teaspoon ground cardamon
1/4 cup sugar, divided
1 (8 ounce) package
   pitted dates cut in halves
1 cup canned sliced apples,
   well-drained

2 cups prepared biscuit mix
2 tablespoons butter or margarine
1 egg, separated
1/3 to 1/2 cup milk

Combine cinnamon and cardamon with 2 tablespoons sugar. Set aside 1 teaspoon of mixture for top of cooked roll. Combine dates and apples. Add spiced sugar mixture and blend well. Add remaining 2 tablespoons sugar to biscuit mix. Cut in batter until mixture resembles coarse meal. Add beaten egg yolk to milk. Stir into dry ingredients, mixing with a fork to form a fairly stiff dough. Knead on a floured board 8 or 10 times. Roll out to 12 by 18 inch rectangle. Brush surface generously with unbeaten egg white. Pile filling in center. Spread to within 2 1/2 inch from long edge and to within 1/4 inches of each end. Fold long edges of dough to center, overlapping and sealing edges. Carefully transfer to lightly greased baking sheet. Place sealed edges underneath. Score top. Bake at 400 degrees for 25 minutes. Remove from oven. Brush generously with remaining egg whites slightly beaten. Sprinkle with reserved spiced sugar. Return to oven for 5 minutes.

Yield: 1-12 inch roll

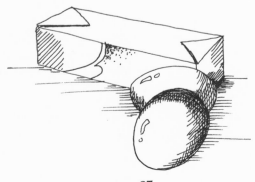

EASY STUFFING

1/2 pound butter or margarine	2 cups water
3/4 cup chopped onion	1 (16 ounce) package herb
1 cup chopped celery	Seasoned stuffing

In a large saucepan, saute the onion and celery in butter until tender but not browned. Stir in water and stuffing. Makes enough to fill a 12 to 16 pound turkey.

CHICKEN OR TURKEY DRESSING

4 cups corn bread crumbs	4 cups loaf bread crumbs,
3 eggs, beaten	fresh, not dried
1 cup buttermilk	1 medium onion, chopped
2 teaspoons poultry seasoning	1/2 teaspoon soda
1/2 teaspoon sage	1 tablespoon butter, melted
1 1/2 cups chicken or turkey	1/4 teaspoon black pepper
broth	Salt to taste

Mix all ingredients together thoroughly. Pour into baking pan and bake at 400 degrees until brown and crisp on top.

Salads

SALADS

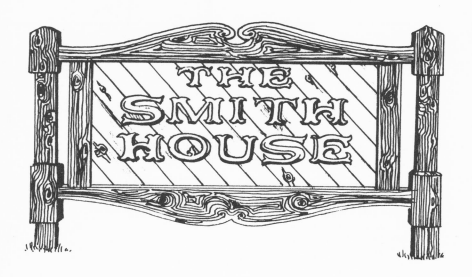

SALADS

TOMATO ASPIC WITH PERSONALITY

1 package lemon flavored
  gelatin
1 1/4 cup boiling water
1 (8 ounce) can tomato sauce
1 1/2 tablespoons vinegar
1/2 teaspoon salt
Dash pepper

Optional - for dash of difference
Dash of onion juice
Dash of celery salt
Dash cayenne pepper
Dash Worcestershire
Dash horseradish
Dash parsley

Dissolve gelatin in boiling water. Add remaining ingredients and pour into mold. Chill.

Yield: 4 to 6 servings.

COLE SLAW

1 head cabbage, shredded
  or chopped
1 cup mayonnaise
1/2 cup sweet pickles

1/4 cup celery, chopped
  fine
3 carrots, grated
Salt and pepper to taste

Mix cabbage and carrots in a large salad bowl and refrigerate. Put mayonnaise and pickles in a container and stir together. Pour the mayonnaise mixture over the slaw and toss. Season with salt and pepper.

THREE WEEK SLAW

3 pounds white cabbage
  finely chopped
2 onions, finely chopped
1 green pepper or green
  tomato, chopped

DRESSING
2 cups sugar
1 cup vegetable oil
1 cup vinegar
1 or 2 tablespoons celery seed

Combine cabbage, onions and green peppers. Combine vegetable oil, vinegar, celery seed and sugar. Bring to a boil and pour over cabbage mixture while hot. Store in the refrigerator.

APPLE-PINEAPPLE SLAW

3 cups shredded crisp cabbage
1 (9 ounce) can pineapple
  tidbits, drained
1 cup diced, unpared apples

1 cup tiny marshmallows
1/2 cup chopped celery
1/2 cup mayonnaise

Combine and toss until mayonnaise coats all ingredients. Serve in lettuce lined dish.

Yield: 4 to 6 servings.

GERMAN COLD SLAW

1 large head cabbage
1 teaspoon salt
2 cups sugar
1 cup vinegar
1/2 cup water

1 bunch celery
1 teaspoon celery seed
1 green pepper
1 red pepper

Chop cabbage and mix with salt. Let stand 1 hour. Press out liquid. Boil together sugar, vinegar, water, celery, celery seed, green pepper, and red pepper. Mix together with cabbage mixture. Store in refrigerator in glass jar. Will keep indefinately.

APPLE SLAW

3 cups shredded cabbage
1 cup unpeeled diced apples
1 cup miniature marshmallows

1 cup chopped celery
1/2 cup mayonnaise
1/2 cup chopped pecans

Combine all ingredients; mixing well.

CRANBERRY SALAD

1 can whole Cranberry
  sauce
1 (3 ounce) package
  strawberry flavored gelatin
1 cup boiling water

1/4 teaspoon salt
1 tablespoon lemon juice
1 apple or orange, chopped
  or 1 (8 ounce) can crushed
  pineapple, drained

Boil water and add gelatin, stirring until dissolved. Mix in cranberry
sauce, salt and lemon juice; add fruit last. If pineapple is used drain
well, squeezing out excess juice. Pour into large casserole and chill until
firm.

CHEESY LEMON MOLD

1 (3 ounce) package lemon-flavored gelatin
1 cup boiling water
1 (6 ounce) can frozen orange juice concentrate
1 (8 ounce) package cream cheese, softened
1 cup flaked coconut
1 cup grated carrots
1 (17 ounce) can crushed pineapple, undrained

Dissolve gelatin in boiling water; Stir in orange juice. Beat cream cheese until smooth and gradually add to gelatin mixture, beating until smooth. Stir in coconut, carrots and pineapple. Pour into a lightly oiled 6 cup mold. Chill until set.

Yield: 10 to 12 servings.

CREAMY FRUIT SALAD

1 (8 3/4 ounce) can fruit
    cocktail, drained
2 bananas, peeled and
    sliced crosswise
1 small unpared apple, diced
1/2 cup seedless green grapes,
    halved

5 maraschino cherries, halved
1/4 cup miniature marshmallows
1/2 cup whipping cream,
    whipped
Strawberries

In large bowl, combine fruit cocktail, bananas, apple, grapes, cherries and marshmallows. Fold in whipped cream; refrigerate. Just before serving, garnish salad with strawberries.

Yield: 4 to 6 servings.

WATERGATE SALAD

1 (20 ounce) can crushed
   pineapple
1 box instant pistachio
   pudding

1/2 cup chopped nuts
3/4 cup small marshmallows
1 (9 ounce) carton frozen whipped
   dessert topping

Combine all the ingredients. Mix well. Chill and serve.

PINEAPPLE SALAD

1 No. 2 can crushed pineapple
1 box orange and pineapple
   flavored gelatin
nuts and cherries, optional

2 (3 ounce) packages
   cream cheese
1 package dry whipped
   topping mix, whipped

Heat pineapple in saucepan and add flavored gelatin; stir until dissolved. Pour over softened cream cheese and mix well. Place in refrigerator until mixture begins to thicken. Mix in whipped cream (nuts and cherries if desired). Return to refrigerator to congeal.

JELL-O-DELITE SALAD

1 (6 ounce) package lime
  flavored gelatin
2 cups boiling water
2 cups Seven-Up

2 cups miniature marshmallows
3 bananas, sliced
1 medium can crushed pineapple,
  drained

TOPPING
2 eggs
2 tablespoons flour
1/2 cup sugar
2 tablespoons butter

1 cup pineapple juice
1 package dry whipped
  topping mix

Dissolve gelatin in boiling water. Cool slightly. Drain pineapple. Reserve juice and add enough water to make 1 cup of liquid. Add 7-up, marshmallows, bananas, and drained pineapple to gelatin. Refrigerate.

Topping: Mix eggs, sugar, and flour. Stir in butter and juice. Cook over medium heat until thick, stirring often. Cool. Prepare dry whipped topping mix according to package directions and fold into cooled cooked mixture. Top gelatin with sauce when ready to serve.

STRAWBERRY SALAD
(GREAT WITH BLUEBERRIES)

1 large package frozen
  strawberries or blueberries
1 (6 ounce) package strawberry
  flavored gelatin
1 small can crushed pineapple
  drained
2 cups boiling water

1 (8 ounce) package cream
  cheese
1 cup sour cream
1/2 cup sugar
1/2 teaspoon vanilla
Nuts

Drain pineapple. Reserve juice and enough water to make 1 cup of liquid. Dissolve gelatin in boiling water and add the cup of juice. Mix in pineapple and strawberries and refrigerate overnight. Combine sour cream, cream cheese, sugar, vanilla, and beat until smooth. Pour evenly over gelatin. Sprinkle top with nuts to garnish.

FRUIT SALAD

8 ounces cottage cheese
2 bananas, sliced
2 apples, diced
1 carrot, grated

1 cup pineapple chunks
drained
1/2 cup pineapple juice

Mix all ingredients together and chill

EASY FRUIT SALAD

1 (9 ounce) carton frozen whipped dessert topping, thawed
1 (6 ounce) package black cherry flavored gelatin
1 can pitted dark sweet cherries, drained well
1 large can crushed pineapple, drained well
1 large carton cottage cheese

Combine all ingredients, chill and serve. The cherries and flavor of gelatin may be replaced with your choice of canned fruit and gelatin. Example - Mandarin oranges and orange flavored gelatin.

Yield: about 15

COCA-COLA SALAD

2 (3 ounce) packages cherry
  flavored gelatin
1 small can crushed
  pineapple, drained
1 can pitted cherries

1 cup chopped pecans
1 cup hot water
2 small cokes (12 ounce)
  total

Dissolve gelatin in boiling water. Mix in pineapple, cherries, and nuts. Pour in Coca-Cola and stir well. Refrigerate overnight.

FIVE CUP SALAD

1 large can pineapple
2 (11 ounce) cans mandarin
  oranges
1 1/2 cups coconut

2 cups miniature marshmallows
1 pint sour cream

Drain pineapple and oranges, then add marshmallows and coconut. Using a wooden spoon, lightly fold in sour cream. Chill and serve.

FROSTY FRUIT SALAD

1 (8 ounce) packages Neufchatel cheese, softened
1 cup sour cream
1/4 cup sugar
1/4 teaspoon salt
1 (17 ounce) can apricot halves, drained and halved
1 (8 3/4 ounce) can crushed pineapple, drained
1 (16 ounce) can pitted dark sweet cherries, drained
1 cup miniature marshmallows

In large mixing bowl, cream cheese until smooth. Blend in sour cream, sugar and salt on low speed. Stir in fruit and marshmallows. Pour into 6 to 8 individual molds or one 4 1/2 cup mold. Freeze at least 8 hours. Ten minutes before serving, unmold on crisp greens.

Yield: 6 to 8 servings.

GOLDEN FRUIT SALAD

3 (3 ounce) packages lemon
  orange flavored gelatin
2 (12 ounce) cans apricot
  nectar

1 (17 ounce) can crushed
  pineapple
1 (11 ounce) can mandarin
  oranges

Heat nect. and fruit juices - add jello. Add enough water to make 4 cups juice. Cool, add fruit and refrigerate.

TOPPING
1/4 tablespoon grated lemon peel
1/4 cup lemon juice
1/4 cup sugar
2 eggs, well beaten

Combine - cook in double boiler until thick. Add above to 1 carton cool or dream whip. Spread on top of gelatin-fruit mixture. Serve in squares.

HOT GERMAN POTATO SALAD

9 medium potatoes, peeled
6 slices bacon
3/4 cup chopped onion
2 tablespoons flour
2 tablespoons sugar
2 teaspoons salt
1/2 teaspoon celery seed

Dash of pepper
3/4 cup water
1/3 cup vinegar
2 (12 ounce) packages of
   Bratwurst sausage
2 tablespoons shortening

In saucepan, heat 1 inch salted water (1/2 teaspoon salt to each 1 cup water) to boiling. Add potatoes, cover and cook 30 to 35 minutes or until tender. Drain and set aside. In a large skillet, fry bacon until crisp; remove and drain. Cook and stir onion in bacon drippings until golden brown. Blend in flour, sugar, salt, celery seed and pepper. Cook over low heat, stirring until mixture is bubbly. Remove from heat. Stir in water and vinegar. Heat to boiling, stirring constantly. Boil and stir 1 minute. Crumble bacon over potatoes which have been thinly sliced. Carefully stir bacon and potatoes into hot mixture. Heat through, stirring lightly to coat potato slices. In skillet brown bratwurst in shortening, turning with tongs; do not pierce with a fork. Serve with potato salad.

Yield: 5 to 6 servings.

GOURMET POTATO SALAD

10 cups diced pared
   cooked potatoes
1 1/2 cups dairy sour cream
1 cup salad dressing

4 teaspoons seasoned salt
1/2 cup chopped dill pickle
1 teaspoon coarsley ground
   pepper

Mix all ingredients except potatoes; pour over potatoes and toss. Cover chill several hours.

Yield: 12 servings.

CHEF'S SALAD

1 head lettuce, washed
  and chilled
1 small head romaine or
  endive, washed and chilled
1 cup julienne strips of
  cooked meat (beef or ham)
1 cup julienne strips of
  cooked chicken or turkey
1 cup julienne strips of
  Swiss cheese

1/2 cup chopped green onions
1/2 cup sliced celery
1 (2 ounce) can anchovy
  fillets, drained
1/2 cup mayonnaise
1/4 cup French dressing
2 hard-cooked eggs, sliced
2 tomatoes, cut in wedges
Olives

Into a large salad bowl, tear lettuce and romaine into bite-size pieces (about 12 cups). Reserve a few strips of meat and cheese. Toss remaining meat, cheese, onion, celery, and anchovies with salad greens. Blend mayonnaise and French dressing; pour over salad and toss. Garnish with reserved meat and cheese strips, the olives, egg slices and tomato wedges.
Yield: 4 large servings.

ENGLISH PEA SALAD

1 can tiny English peas
1 can French cut green beans
1 small jar pimiento

4 stalks celery, chopped
1 medium onion, sliced and
  separate in rings

DRESSING
3/4 cup apple cider vinegar
1/2 cup salad oil

1 cup sugar

Mix dressing and pour over vegetables. Marinate overnight in refrigerator before serving.

CUCUMBERS IN SOUR CREAM

2 medium cucumbers, peeled
  thinly sliced
1 medium onion, sliced
1 teaspoon salt
1 cup dairy sour cream

1/4 to 1/3 cup Apple Cider
  vinegar
1 tablespoon sugar
Paprika

Combine onion, cucumbers, and salt. Cover and chill. Combine vinegar, sour cream, and sugar. Cover and chill. Just before serving drain cubumbers well and blend into the sour cream dressing. Garnish with paprika.

Yield: 6 to 8 servings.

LETTUCE AND BOILED EGG SALAD

1/2 head lettuce, broken
  in pieces

2 medium onions, sliced in rings
6 hard boiled eggs, sliced

DRESSING
1/2 cup mayonnaise
1 tablespoon prepared mustard
2 tablespoons vinegar

1/2 teaspoon pepper
1 teaspoon salt

Combine lettuce, onions and eggs in salad bowl. Mix dressing ingreidents and pour over lettuce and toss.

AMBROSIA MOLD

1 (3 ounce) package orange
  pineapple flavored gelatin
1 tablespoon sugar
1 cup boiling water
3/4 cup cold water
2/3 cup flaked coconut

2 oranges, peeled and
  sectioned
1 1/4 cup seedless grapes,
  halved
1 cup whipping cream,
  whipped

Dissolve gelatin and sugar in boiling water; stir in cold water. Chill until partially set. Stir in oranges, grapes, and coconut; fold in whipped cream. Pour into a lightly oiled 6-cup mold; chill until set.

Yield: 6 to 8 servings.

VALENTINE SALAD

2 cups crushed pineapple
1 1/2 tablespoons unflavored
  gelatin
2 tablespoons marschino
  cherry juice
12 marschino cherries, chopped

1/2 cup sugar
1/4 cup cold water
2 (3 ounce) packages cream
  cheese
1/2 pint whipping cream

Soften gelatin with 1/4 cup of water. Heat pineapple with sugar and add gelatin and cherry juice. Cool. Soften and mash cream cheese and add finely chopped cherries. Add pineapple to cream cheese, mixing a small amoung in at a time. Whip until slightly thickened. Whip cream and blend into pineapple mixture. Pour into mold and chill.

Meats

MEAT

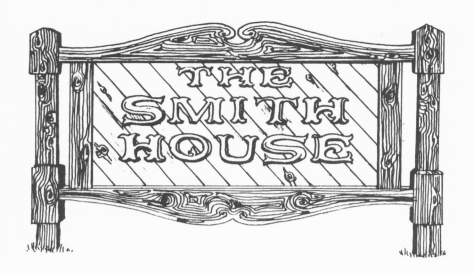

MEATS

STEAK WITH RICE

1 pound tenderized round
  steak, cut in thin strips
1/4 teaspoon garlic powder
1 large onion, sliced
1 tablespoon vegetable oil
1 large green pepper, sliced
1 cup celery, cut in 1 inch
  pieces
1 (14 ounce) can tomatoes,
  quartered

1/2 cup beef broth
1 cup drained cubed
  pineapple
1 teaspoon ginger
2 teaspoons sugar
2 tablespoons cornstarch
1/3 cup soy sauce
3 cups hot cooked rice

Sprinkle steak with garlic powder and saute in oil until browned. Add onion, green pepper, and celery. Cook about 1 minute. Stir in tomatoes, broth, pineapple, ginger and sugar. Cover and simmer 5 minutes. Blend cornstarch into soy sauce and stir into meat mixture. Cook until lightly glazed about 1 minute. Serve over beds of fluffy rice.

Yield: 6 servings.

COLA ROAST

1 beef roast, (a bottom round, chuck or other less tender cut works well
12 ounce cola drink
1 package dry onion soup mix

Place unseasoned roast in baking dish. Sprinkle with onion soup mix Pour in cola drink. Cover and seal tightly with aluminum foil. Roast in oven at 300 degrees until tender. Time will vary with size of roast. A 4 pound roast will take 3½ to 4 hours.

ROAST BEEF WITH BARBECUE SAUCE
Great for Leftover Roast

1/2 cup wine vinegar	1 cup meat stock
2 cloves garlic, quartered	1 tablespoon Worcestershire
1 teaspoon dry mustard	1 tablespoon butter
1 teaspoon paprika	1/8 teaspoon cayenne
12 peppercorns	Thin slice roast beef
1 cup tomato sauce	4 toasted buns

Cook vinegar, garlic, mustard, paprika, cayenne and peppercorns 5 minutes; strain. Heat tomato sauce and stock and add strained spice mixture. Add Worcestershire sauce and butter. Cook 3 minutes. Add roast and cook 15 minutes. Serve on toasted buns.

Yield: 4 servings

POT ROAST WITH SOUR CREAM GRAVY

2 1/2 pound beef chuck
  pot-roast
2 tablespoons flour
2 teaspoons salt, divided
1/4 teaspoon pepper
1 tablespoon shortening

1 tablespoon vinegar
1 teaspoon dill weed
5 small potaotes, pared
5 carrots, quartered
1 pound zucchini, quartered
1/4 cup water

SOUR CREAM GRAVY
Roast drippings
1 tablespoon flour
Water

1 cup sour cream
Salt and pepper
1 teaspoon dill weed

Combine flour, 1 teaspoon salt and the pepper; coat meat with flour mixture. Melt shortening in large skillet or Dutch oven and brown meat. Add water, vinegar and sprinkle dill weed over the meat.
Cover tightly and simmer about 3 hours or until meat is tender. One hour before end of cooking time, add potatoes and carrots; season with 1/2 teaspoon of salt. 20 minutes before end of cooking time add zucchini; season with 1/2 teaspoon salt. Serve with Sour Cream Gravy.

Yield 4 to 6 servings

GRAVY: Place meat and vegetables on warm platter. Pour drippings from pan into bowl, leaving brown particles in pan. Return 1 tablespoon drippings to pan. Blend in 1 tablespoon flour. Cook over low heat, stirring until mixture is smooth and bubbly. Remove from heat. Measure drippings and add enough water to measure 1 cup liquid. Stir into flour mixture. Heat to boiling, stirring constantly. Boil and stir 1 minute. Season with salt and pepper. Stir in sour cream and dill weed; heat through.

Yield: 2 cups

49

HEARTY BEEF STEW

2 pounds stew meat
  cut in 1 1/2 inch cubes
4 cups water
1/4 cup chopped onion
1 bay leaf
1/4 teaspoon pepper
6 medium carrots, pared and
  cut in 1-inch pieces
1/4 cup water

1/4 cup all-purpose flour
1/4 cup all-vegetable shortening
1 (8 ounce) can tomato sauce
1/2 teaspoon garlic salt
2 teaspoons salt
6 medium potatoes, pared and
  quartered
3 medium onions, quartered
1/4 cup cornstarch

BISCUITS

2 cups flour
3 teaspoons baking powder
1 teaspoon salt

1/3 cup shortening
3/4 cup milk

Coat meat with four and brown in hot shortening in a Dutch oven. Add 4 cups water, tomato sauce, chopped onion, garlic salt, bay leaf, salt and pepper. Bring to a boil, then reduce heat. Cover and simmer 1 1/2 to 2 hours, or until meat is tender. Add potatoes, carrots and quartered onions; cover and simmer until vegetables are tender about 1/2 hour. Blend cornstarch and 1/4 cup water; add to stew and stir until mixture boils. Simmer 5 minutes. Place stew in large, shallow baking dish or pan and top with biscuits. Bake in 425 degree oven 20 to 25 minutes.

BISCUITS: Combine flour, baking powder and salt in bowl. Cut in shortening until mixture resembles coarse meal. Add milk and stir just enough to moisten well. Knead dough 8 to 10 times on lightly floured surface. Roll or pat out to 1/2 inch thickness. Cut into 2-inch biscuits.

BRUNSWICK STEW

3 pounds cut-up squirrel
  rabbit or chicken
1/4 cup cooking oil
2 onions, sliced
2 (29 ounce) cans tomatoes
1/2 bay leaf
1 teaspoon chopped parsley
Pinch of thyme
1 cup water

1 tablespoon salt
Pepper to taste
2 (10 ounce) packages, frozen,
  cut corn
1 (10 ounce) package frozen
  lima beans
2 tablespoons cornstarch
1/3 cup cold water

Brown meat in oil in Dutch oven or sauce pan. Remove meat. Brown onions in remaining oil. Return meat to pan. Add tomatoes, bay leaf, parsley, thyme, water and salt. When bubbling, cover. Reduce heat. Simmer 1 hour. Add corn and lima beans. Simmer 30 minutes more. Dissolve cornstarch in water. Add to stew, stirring gently, until stew is slightly thickened and clear. Season to taste.

Yield: 8 to 12 servings.

EXCELLENT SOUTHERN STEW

1 1/4 pounds ground fresh pork
1 can tomatoes
1 can corn
3 large onions, chopped fine
3 tablespoons catsup

1 tablespoon Worcestershire
1 tablespoon sugar
Salt to taste
1/2 cup bread crumbs

Brown pork in skillet. Put tomatoes, corn and onions in sauce pan. Add browned pork, catsup, Worcestershire sauce, sugar, and salt. Cook 20 minutes. Add bread crumbs and serve hot.

STEAK CASSEROLE

1 1/2 pounds round steak
1 pound mushrooms or
  1 can mushrooms
1 small onion, chopped

1 cup tomato juice
1 can English peas
Flour, salt and pepper

Cut steak into serving pieces and pound salt, pepper and flour into it. Sear quickly in skillet with oil and then put into covered baking dish. Add peas, mushrooms, onion and tomato juice. Cook 2 hours in oven at 300 degrees.

PIRATE STEAK

3 pound sirloin steak
  1 1/2 to 2 inches thick
1 (12 ounce) can beer
1/2 cup chili sauce
1/4 cup salad oil
2 tablespoons soy sauce
1/2 teaspoon red pepper sauce

1 tablespoon dijon type
  mustard
1/8 teaspoon liquid smoke
1/2 cup chopped onions
2 cloves, garlic, crushed
1 teaspoon salt
1/2 teaspoon pepper

Mix all ingredients together except salt, pepper, and steak; simmer 30 minutes. Brush meat with sauce. Place steak on grill 4 inches from medium coals. Cook 15 minutes on each side, basting frequently with sauce. Season with salt and pepper after removing steak from grill.

PEPPER STEAK

1 1/2 pound top round
   steak 3/4 to 1 inch thick
1/4 cup salad oil
1 cup water
1 medium onion, cut into
   1/4 inch slices
1/2 teaspoon garlic salt
1/4 teaspoon ginger

2 medium green peppers,
   cut into 3/4 inch strips
1 tablespoon cornstarch
2 to 3 teaspoons sugar
2 tablespoons soy sauce
2 medium tomatoes
Hot cooked rice

Trim fat from meat and cut meat into strips, 2x1/4 inch. Heat oil in large skillet and brown the meat. Turn often. (This takes about 5 minutes). Stir in water, onion, garlic salt and ginger. Heat to boiling. Reduce heat; cover and simmer 12 to 15 minutes for round steak, 5 to 8 minutes for sirloin. Add green pepper strips during last 5 minutes of simmering.

Blend mixture of cornstarch, sugar and soy sauce and stir into meat mixture. Cook, stirring constantly, until mixture thickens and boils. Boil and stir 1 minute. Cut each tomato into eights; and place on meat mixture. Cover and cook over low heat until tomatoes are heated through - about 3 minutes. Serve over hot rice.

Yield: 4 to 5 servings

LONDON BROIL

2 pounds high-quality flank
  steak, scored
1 tablespoon margarine
2 medium onions, thinly sliced
1/4 teaspoon salt

2 tablespoons salad oil
1 teaspoon lemon juice
2 cloves garlic, crushed
1/2 teaspoon salt, divided
1/4 teaspoon pepper

Saute onions in oil until tender; add 1/4 teaspoon salt while stirring. Keep warm, over low heat. Combine salad oil, lemon juice, garlic, 1/2 teaspoon salt and pepper; brush on top side of meat. Broil meat 2 to 3 inches from heat until brown, approximately 5 minutes. Turn meat, brush with oil mixture and broil until rare, about 5 minutes longer. Cut meat across the grain at a slanted angle into very thin slices. Serve with onions.

STEAK AND MUSHROOM

1/2 cup sliced mushrooms
2 tablespoons minced onion
1/8 teaspoon salt
1 teaspoon lemon juice
1 teaspoon Worcestershire

1/4 cup butter or margarine
2 tablespoons snipped parsley
2 tablespoons butter
1 pound beef tenderloin,
  cut into 8 slices

Cook mushrooms, onion and seasonings in 1/4 cut butter until mushrooms are tender. Stir in parsley; keep sauce warm. Melt 2 tablespoons butter in skillet. Turning once, cook meat in butter over medium-high heat to medium doneness, 3 to 4 minutes on each side. Serve with mushroom sauce.

Yield: 4 servings.

FAVORITE MEAT LOAF

1/2 pound ground pork
1 pound ground beef
1/2 pound ground veal
2 teaspoons salt
1/4 teaspoon pepper
4 slices bread or toast
   broken in pieces

1 cup warm milk
2 eggs, beaten
1/4 cup minced onion
1 tablespoon salad oil
2 cups canned tomatoes
1 bouillon cube
1/2 cup hot water

Soften bread in milk and add eggs, onions, meats, salt and pepper. Mix thoroughly and shape into a loaf. Place in greased pan. Spread with salad oil and then tomatoes. Dissolve bouillon in hot water and then pour around loaf. Bake in a moderate oven, 350 degrees for 1 1/2 to 2 hours. Baste every 15 minutes.

Yield: 6.

MEAT LOAF II

1 pound ground beef
1/2 cup dry bread crumbs
   or Quaker oats
1/4 teaspoon pepper
1 teaspoon accent
1 egg beaten

1 small onion, chopped fine
3/4 teaspoon salt
1/2 teaspoon thyme
1/2 cup milk
1 can mushroom soup

Mix all ingredients except soup. Shape into a loaf. Place in shallow pan and bake at 350 degrees for 45 minutes. Pour can of mushroom soup over loaf and bake 15 minutes longer.

Yield: 5 to 6 servings.

HAWAIIAN BURGERS

1 1/2 pounds ground meat
1 1/2 teaspoons salt
1/4 teaspoon pepper
1 (13 ounce) can pineapple
  tidbits, drained
2 cloves garlic, minced

1/4 cup salad oil
1/4 cup soy sauce
2 tablespoons catsup
1 tablespoon vinegar
1/4 teaspoon pepper
6 slices bacon

Mix thoroughly the meat, salt, and 1/4 teaspoon pepper. Shape into 6 patties and press 5 to 6 pineapple tidbits into each. Combine garlic, oil, soy sauce, catsup, vinegar and pepper. Place patties in glass dish and pour oil mixture over patties. Cover; refrigerate 30 minutes, turning occasionally. Remove patties from marinade. Wrap a bacon slice around each patty and secure with wooden toothpick. Cook patties on rack in broiler pan about 5 inches from heat with oven set on broil or 550 degrees for 12 to 15 minutes. These can be cooked on a grill.

Yield: 6 servings.

DOUBLE CHEESE DELIGHT

1 pound ground beef
4 ounces uncooked medium
  noodles
1/3 cup chopped onion
1 tablespoon chopped celery
1 (8 ounce) can tomato sauce
1 teaspoon salt

1/2 cup creamed cottage
  cheese
1 (3 ounce) package cream
  cheese, softened
1/4 cup sour cream
1 medium tomato

Cook noodles as directed on package. Drain. In large skillet, brown ground beef, and cook onion and celery until tender. Drain. Stir in tomato sauce and salt. Bring to a boil, reduce heat and simmer 1 minute. Remove from heat. Stir in cottage cheese, cream cheese, sour cream and noodles. Pour into ungreased 1 1/2-quart casserole. Arrange sliced tomato on top. Cover. Bake 350 degrees for 30 minutes.

Yield 4 servings.

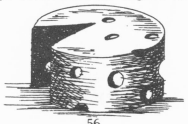

BARBECUED PATTIES

1/2 pound ground round steak
1/2 cup soft bread crumbs
1/4 cup milk
1/2 teaspoon salt
Dash of pepper

2 tablespoons shortening
1 tablespoon Worcestershire
1 tablespoon sugar
1 tablespoon cider vinegar
1/2 cup tomato catsup

Moisten crumbs with milk. Add meat, salt and pepper. Form in 6 patties and brown in shortening. Combine the worcestershire, sugar, vinegar, and catsup and pour over the patties. Cover and simmer slowly about 10 or 15 minutes, or until sauce is thick. Serve between hot toasted buns.

STUFFED GREEN PEPPERS

3 large green peppers
1/2 teaspoon salt
1/2 pound ground beef
1 cup dry bread crumbs
   or cracker crumbs

1 tablespoon chopped onion
1 teaspoon salt
1/4 teaspoon pepper
1 (8 ounce) can tomato sauce

Cut thin slice from stem end of each pepper. Remove all seeds. Wash inside and outside. Boil 1 cup water and 1/2 teaspoon salt. Add peppers and cook 5 minutes. Drain. Mix remaining ingredients. Lightly stuff each pepper with 1/3 of the meat mixture. Stand peppers upright in ungreased baking dish, 8x8x2 inches. Cover; bake 350 degrees for 45 minutes. Uncover; bake 15 minutes longer.

Yield: 3 servings

BEEF STROGANOFF

2 pounds round steak, cut
  in long narrow strips
6 tablespoons flour
1 teaspoon salt
1/4 teaspoon pepper
2 teaspoons dry mustard
2 cups water

1 onion, sliced
1 (4 ounce) can of mushroom
  pieces
1 can cream of mushroom soup
1/2 teaspoon salt
1 cup sour cream

Dredge meat in flour, salt and pepper mixture and brown in small amount of fat or bacon drippings. Add 2 cups water, dry mustard, salt and pepper, sliced onion and the can of mushroom soup. Make a paste of 2 tablespoons flour and 2 tablespoons of water and slowly add to meat mixture, stirring constantly to avoid lumping. Simmer until gravy is thick and smooth.
Stir in 1 cup sour cream and bring to boiling point over low heat but do not boil. Serve over hot rice.

VEGETABLE MEAT PIE

1 pound ground beef
1 cup soft bread crumbs
1 egg, beaten
1 (8 ounce) can tomato sauce,
  divided
1 teaspoon chili powder
Dash cayenne

1 (10 ounce) package frozen
  mixed vegetables, or a 1 pound
  can mixed vegetables, drained
1 teaspoon garlic salt
1/2 cup grated sharp process
  American cheese
1 teaspoon salt

Combine meat, bread crumbs, beaten eggs, 1/3 cup of tomato sauce, salt, chili powder and cayenne. Press into 9 inch pieplate, building up edges. Pour boiling water over frozen vegetables to separate. Drain well. Season with garlic salt. Fill meat shell with vegetables and pour remaining tomato sauce over. Bake in moderate oven, 350 degrees for 25 minutes. Sprinkle grated cheese on top and bake 5 minutes longer, or till cheese melts. Garnish with parsley.

Yield: 4 to 6 servings

SPAGHETTI-CHEESE CASSEROLE

1 (7 ounce) package spaghetti
1 (number 2) can tomatoes
1/2 cup chopped onions
1/2 cup chopped celery

1 teaspoon salt
1 teaspoon Worcestershire
1/2 teaspoon oregano
1 cup grated Cheddar cheese

Cook spaghetti until tender. Cook tomatoes, onion, celery and seasonings together for 15 minutes. Combine spaghetti, sauce and cheese. Pour into buttered 1 1/2 quart casserole. Top with additional grated cheese. Bake in 350 degree oven for 30 minutes.

Yield: 4 servings

NOODLE AND BEEF CASSEROLE

1 1/2 pounds lean ground beef
6 ounces egg noodles
  cooked and drained
2 tablespoons bacon drippings
1 green pepper, chopped
1 stalk celery, chopped
1 large onion, chopped
1 teaspoon salt

1 teaspoon pepper
1 tablespoon sugar
1 teaspoon chili powder
1 can tomato soup
1 can mushroom soup
3/4 cup water
1 cup grated cheese

Cook noodles and drain. Saute pepper, celery, and onions in bacon drippings. Add meat and cook until pink color is gone. Mix noodles and meat mixture well. Add salt and pepper, sugar, chili powder, soups, and water and mix well. Pour in casserole and top with grated cheese. Bake at 350 degrees for 45 minutes.

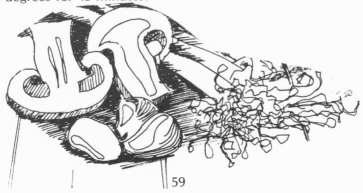

CHEESEBURGER PIE

1 (9 inch) pastry pie shell
1 pound ground beef
1 teaspoon salt
1/2 teaspoon oregano
1/4 teaspoon pepper
1/2 cup dry bread crumbs

1 (8 ounce) can tomato sauce,
    divided
1/4 cup chopped onion
1/4 cup chopped green pepper
1/2 cup chili sauce

CHEESE TOPPING
1/4 cup milk
1 egg
1/2 teaspoon salt
1/2 teaspoon Worcestershire

1/2 teaspoon dry mustard
2 cups shredded Cheddar cheese
    about 8 ounces

Prepare pastry for 9 inch pie. In medium skillet, cook and stir meat until brown. Drain off fat. Stir in salt, oregano, pepper, crumbs, 1/2 cup tomato sauce, onion, and green pepper. Turn into pastry-lined pie pan. Make cheese topping; beat egg and milk, stir in salt, worcestershire, dry mustard and cheese. Spread over meat filling. Bake about 30 minutes in preheated 425 degree oven. Stir together remaining tomato sauce and chili sauce; serve with pie.

Yield: 6 to 8 servings

PICADILLO
(pronounced p-k-d-yo)

2 pounds ground meat
1 onion, chopped
1 green pepper, chopped
1 clove garlic
1 small can tomato sauce

1 teaspoon capers
1/2 cup raisins
1 small bottle stuffed olives
2 teaspoons salt

Saute onion, green pepper, and garlic in a little fat. When tender, add ground meat and brown. Add tomato sauce, capers, and raisins and let simmer slightly. When Picadillo is nearly done, add stuffed olives. Serve over hot rice.

SWEDISH MEATBALLS

1/4 pound fresh pork, ground
1 1/4 pound ground beef
1 egg, slightly beaten
1 cup milk
1/4 cup fine dry bread crumbs
2 tablespoons minced onions

3 tablespoons margarine
1 1/2 teaspoons salt
1/2 teaspoon pepper
2 tablespoons plain flour
1 cup hot water
3/4 cup light cream

Combine egg, milk and bread crumbs. Let stand for a few minutes. Brown onions in 1 tablespoon of margarine and then combine with soaked crumbs, ground beef, pork, salt and pepper. Mix with a spoon until smooth. Shape into 3 dozen balls about 1 inch in diameter and brown in remaining margarine. Pour off most of the fat and then sprinkle meatballs with flour. Add hot water, cover and simmer for 35 to 40 minutes, then add cream.

MEATBALL MINIATURES

1/2 pound ground beef
2 sliced dry bread
1 egg
1/4 cup grated Romano cheese
1 tablespoon chopped parsley

1 clove garlic, minced
1/2 teaspoon crushed oregano
1/2 teaspoon salt
Dash of pepper

Soak bread in water 2 or 3 minutes. Then squeeze out the moisture. Combine soaked bread with remaining ingredients, mixing well. Shape into tiny 1/2 inch meat balls. Brown slowly in butter, shaking skillet to keep balls round.
Spear with tooth picks. Serve hot with cocktail sauce.

SPAGHETTI WITH MEAT SAUCE OR MEATBALLS

ITALIAN MEAT SAUCE

1 pound ground beef
1/2 cup onion, chopped
1/2 cup green pepper, chopped
2 tablespoons salad oil
2 cloves garlic, minced
4 cups tomatoes
2 (8 ounce) cans seasoned
  tomato sauce
1/4 cup chopped parsley

1 (3 ounce) can broiled sliced
  mushrooms
1 1/2 teaspoon oregano
1 teaspoon salt
1/2 teaspoon Accent
1/4 teaspoon thyme
1 bay leaf
1 cup water

Add oil to large skillet and cook onion and pepper until wilted. Add meat and garlic and lightly brown. Add remaining ingredients. Simmer uncovered 2 to 2 1/2 hours or until sauce is nice and thick. Stir occasionally. Remove bay leaf. Serve hot over hot spaghetti. Serve with shredded Parmesan cheese. One pound of spaghetti will serve 4 to 6 people as the main dish with sauce.

Yield: 6 servings

VEAL PARMIGIAN

1 pound thin veal cutlets
cut into 8 pieces - about
4 1/2 by 2 inches
Olive or salad oil
3 garlic cloves, finely
minced
1 onion, minced
1 (16 ounce) can tomatoes
1 1/4 teaspoon salt
1/4 teaspoon pepper

1 (8 ounce) can tomato sauce
1/4 teaspoon thyme
1 egg
1/4 cup packaged dried
bread crumbs
1/2 cup grated Parmesan
cheese, divided
1/2 pound Mozzarella or
Muenster cheese

About 1 hour before serving saute onion and garlic in 3 tablespoons of oil until golden. Add tomatoes, salt and pepper. Break tomatoes apart with spoon and simmer uncovered for 10 minutes. Add tomato sauce and thyme and simmer uncovered 20 minutes more. Beat egg well with fork. Combine bread crumbs and 1/4 cup of the Parmesan cheese. Dip each piece of veal into egg then into crumb mixture and cook in 1 tablespoon of hot oil. Saute a few pieces at a time until golden brown on both sides. Arrange slices in 12x8x2 inch baking dish. Place thinly sliced Mozzarella on top of veal pieces and spoon tomato mixture over. Sprinkle with 1/4 cup Parmesan. Bake, uncovered in a preheated 350 degree oven for 30 minutes or until fork tender.

Yield: 4 generous servings

SAUSAGE CASSEROLE

1 pound sausage
1 small can mushrooms,
drained
1 envelope dry chicken
noodle soup mix
1/2 cup celery, chopped fine
1 1/2 cups water

3 cups cooked rice
1 can celery soup
1 onion, chopped fine
1 green pepper, chopped fine
1/4 cup water chestnuts
(chopped)
Salt and pepper to taste

Cook sausage until all pink is gone, stirring constantly so that none will brown. Drain well. Par boil onions, celery and green peppers for a few minutes. Drain. Mix all ingredients together. Bake at 350 for 1 hour or a little longer if it appears to be too moist. Freezes well.

HAM SLICES AND RED EYE GRAVY

Ham slices 1/4 inch thick   1/4 cup strong black coffee
1/4 cup water

Cut slits in fat around ham slices to prevent curling. Brown ham in heavy skillet, turning several times. Cook slowly until ham is browned. Add water and let ham simmer for a few minutes. Remove ham from skillet and add strong coffee to pan drippings. Bring to a boil. Serve with grits.

POLISH SAUSAGE AND POTATO CASSEROLE

1 pound Kielbasa or Polish   3 tablespoons flour
  sausage, cut in 1/4 inch   2 cups milk
  slices   1/2 teaspoon salt
2 pounds potatoes, peeled   1/4 teaspoon pepper
  cooked and thinly sliced   1 1/2 tablespoons dijon mustard
1/4 cup butter or margarine   2 cups shredded Swiss cheese
1 cup chopped onion   Chopped parsley (optional)

Melt butter in medium saucepan and saute onions until tender. With wire whisk blend in flour. Slowly add milk, stirring until mixture comes to a boil and thickens. Add salt, pepper and mustard. Remove from heat and stir in 1 1/2 cups cheese. In greased 12x8 inch baking dish, arrange half the potatoes and sausage (in a single layer, alternating pieces). Pour over half the sauce, then layer remaining potatoes and sausage. Pour on remaining sauce and sprinkle with 1/2 cup cheese. Bake in a preheated 350 degree oven uncovered 45 to 60 minutes or until top browns and center is heated through. Sprinkle with chopped parsley if desired.

Yield: 8 servings

HAM LOAF

1 pound cured ham, ground
1 pound fresh pork, ground
2 eggs
2/3 cup cracker crumbs
1 1/4 cup milk

1/3 cup minute tapioca
1/2 cup water
1/4 cup vinegar
1 tablespoon mustard
1/2 cup brown sugar

Mix ham, pork, eggs, crumbs, milk and tapioca and shape into a loaf. Combine water, vinegar, mustard and sugar; pour over loaf. Bake at 350 degrees for 2 hours.

Yield: 8 servings

HAM AND EGG CROQUETTES

1 1/2 cups cooked ham, ground
1/2 cup flour
1/3 cup butter
1 1/2 cups milk
4 eggs, hard boiled

Salt and pepper
1 egg
2 tablespoons milk
Dried crumbs

Melt butter in double boiler, add flour and mix well. Add milk gradually and cook, stirring constantly until thickened. Add ham, chopped eggs, salt and pepper to taste. Chill thoroughly and shape into 12 small rolls or balls. Slightly beat egg and mix in milk. Dip balls into egg mixture, roll in crumbs and fry in deep fat at 390 degrees until golden brown. Drain on paper towel.

Yields 6 servings.

GLAZED HAM

1 (6 to 7 pound) ham uncooked **1 (6 ounce) can frozen orange**
1 cup brown sugar, packed **juice concentrate.**

Place ham in pan, fat side up. Combine sugar and orange concentrate; pour about half of mixture over ham. Cover loosely with foil and bake at 325 degrees 30 minutes to the pound.
About 30 minutes before ham is done, remove from oven. Score fat and spoon remaining mixture over ham. Return to oven and bake 30 minutes uncovered at 400 degrees.

PORK CHOP CASSEROLE

6 to 8 pork chops **1 package dry onion soup mix**
1 cup regular rice **3 cups water**

Lightly brown pork chops in skillet. Pour uncooked rice and soup mix in bottom of large shallow casserole. Place chops on top and add water. Cover tightly with foil and bake at 350 degrees for 45 minutes to 1 hour.

HAM STUFFED APPLES

4 large red apples, unpeeled
1 cup baked ham, diced
1/4 cup raisins

1/4 cup chopped pecans
2 tablespoons sugar
2 tablespoons butter

GLAZE
4 tablespoons water
4 tablespoons brown sugar

1 teaspoon dry mustard
2 tablespoons vinegar

Scoop out the apples, leaving thick enough shell to hold stuffing. Mix 1 cup chopped apple with ham, raisins, pecans, sugar and butter. Fill apple cavities with stuffing. Place apples in baking dish.

In sauce pan mix all glaze ingredients; bring to a boil. Spoon the hot glaze over apples and bake in a 350 degree preheated oven for 45 minutes. While apples are baking, baste often with glaze.

Yield: 4 servings

BARBECUED SPARERIBS

8-10 pounds spareribs
water

Cook in water for 1 hour.

SAUCE

1 cup catsup
3 cups vinegar
1/4 cup sugar
1/4 pound butter

1/4 cup hot pepper sauce
1/4 cup salt
1/4 cup Worcestershire sauce

Combine all ingredients and bring to a boil. Pour over ribs and bake for 30 minutes at 375 degrees.   Yield: 15 servings.

LEMON BARBECUED SPARERIBS

3 to 4 pounds spareribs, cut
  into serving-size pieces
1/2 cup lemon juice
1/3 cup catsup
2 teaspoons Worcestershire

1 teaspoon salt
1/4 teaspoon chili powder
1/4 cup brown sugar, packed
1 clove of garlic, minced
1 lemon, thinly sliced

Heat oven to 450. Place ribs in roasting pan. Bake 30 minutes or until meat is lightly browned. Remove from oven. Reduce heat to 350. Drain fat from meat. Combine lemon juice, catsup, Worcestershire, salt, chili powder, brown sugar, and garlic and mix well. Brush spareribs generously with sauce. Place a lemon on each piece of meat. Return meat to oven; bake one hour or until tender, basting frequently with sauce.

Yield: 4 servings.

Poultry

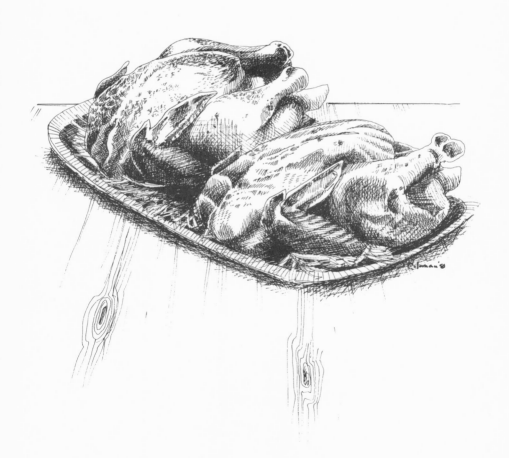

POULTRY

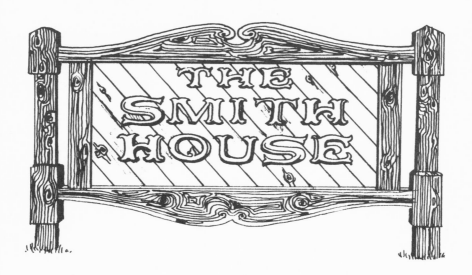

POULTRY

SMITH HOUSE FAMOUS
SOUTHERN FRIED CHICKEN

1 fryer, cut into serving pieces Buttermilk	Self rising flour Cooking oil or shortening

Salt and pepper chicken pieces, dip in buttermilk and roll in flour. Fry in deep fat at 300 degrees until chicken is tender and golden, about 15 minutes. Turn only once.

SOUTHERN FRIED CHICKEN

1 fryer, cut into serving
   size pieces
1 egg
Milk

Flour
Salt and pepper
Cooking oil or shortening
Butter, optional

Beat egg and milk together. Salt chicken pieces, dip in egg mixture and then dredge in a mixture of flour, salt and pepper. (A good way to coat the pieces evenly is to put flour mixture in a bag, add 1 or 2 chicken pieces and shake vigorously.) Deep fry in oil with a little butter added at 300 degrees until chicken is tender and golden brown. Approximately 15 minutes. The butter is not necessary, just adds a little extra flavor.

FAMILY CHICKEN PIE

1 3 to 4 pound chicken
1 can peas and carrots
1/2 cup diced celery
1/2 cup diced onions
3 hard cooked eggs, sliced

1/2 teaspoon salt
1/8 teaspoon pepper
2 tablespoons flour
1 pastry recipe

Boil chicken in water until tender. Remove bones. Cut chicken into small pieces and reserve broth. Combine vegetables, eggs, salt and pepper. Mix flour into small amount of broth and stir until smooth. Add chicken and vegetable mixture to remaining chicken broth. Bring to a boil. Add flour mixture and cook until thickened. Place in shallow oblong baking dish. Roll out pastry to fit baking dish and place over chicken mixture. Bake at 350 degrees for 50 minutes or until golden brown.

CRUSTY CHICKEN PIE

1 - 3 pound fryer
2 eggs, hard boiled
1 stick margarine
Pastry
3/4 cup flour

1/2 teaspoon baking powder
1/4 teaspoon pepper
1 cup milk
·1 egg
1 1/2 cups chicken stock

Cook chicken in salted water until tender. Remove meat from bones and chop. Simmer stock down to 1 1/2 cups. Melt margarine in deep pie pan. Combine flour, baking powder, pepper, milk and 1 egg. Pour this thin batter into dish. Top this with the chicken meat, 2 hard cooked eggs, sliced, and the stock. Bake at 350 degrees for about 1 hour. The thin batter will rise and form a brown crusty topping.

Yield: 6 servings

CHICKEN PIE

1 large fryer
4 cups water
4 eggs, hard boiled

1/2 stick butter
Salt and pepper to taste

CRUST
1 cup water
3 tablespoons shortening
Flour

Cook fryer in water until tender. Remove chicken from bones. Return meat to broth and add eggs, butter and seasoning. For crust, mix water and shortening with enough flour to make a stiff dough   Roll dough out thin and cut into strips. Add a few strips of the dough in the stock and boil. Pour into baking dish, top with strips of dough, dot with butter and brown in oven at 400 degrees.

BUTTERMILK BAKED CHICKEN

1 cut-up fryer
1 1/2 cups buttermilk, divided
3/4 cup flour
1/4 teaspoon pepper

1/4 cup butter or margarine
1 1/2 teaspoon salt
1 can cream of chicken soup

Dip chicken into 1/2 cup buttermilk, roll in flour seasoned with salt and pepper. Melt butter in a 13 by 9 by 2 inch pan. Place chicken in pan, skin side down. Bake uncovered at 425 degrees, for 30 minutes. Turn chicken and bake an additional 15 minutes. Mix remaining 1 cup buttermilk and soup and pour around chicken. Bake 14 minutes more or until drumstick is tender when pierced with a fork.

Yield: 6 servings

CHICKEN BAKED IN MUSHROOM SOUP

6 chicken breast
  or other preferred pieces
1/3 cup cream

1 can cream of mushroom soup
Salt

Salt chicken and saute in butter over quick heat. Arrange pieces in casserole. Combine soup and cream and pour over chicken. Cover casserole and cook for 1 hour in a 325 degree preheated oven. Serve over rice.

CHICKEN BAKE

2 or 3 cups diced chicken
1 stick butter
2 cups chicken broth
2 cups milk

Salt and pepper to taste
1 package stuffing mix
2 eggs
Diced onion (optional)

Melt butter and combine all ingredients, mixing well. Put in casserole and bake in 350 degree oven for 45 minutes.

HERB BAKED CHICKEN IN FOIL

1 fryer, quartered
1 teaspoon grated lemon peel
2 tablespoons fresh lemon juice
1/4 teaspoon dried sweet basil
  leaves crushed

1/4 teaspoon oregano leaves,
  crushed
1 (10 1/2 ounce) can
  cream of mushroom soup

Wash and dry chicken pieces. Place each quarter on a piece of heavy duty foil about 18x14 inches. Mix lemon peel, lemon juice and herbs with mushroom soup. Spoon over chicken. Fold foil snugly over chicken quarters, sealing well so steam will not escape. Bake at 400 degrees, 1 1/4 to 1 1/2 hours. Open and serve in foil.

Yield: 4 servings

75

CHICKEN SIMPLICITY

1 fryer, cut up
1/2 package dry onion soup
1 cup regular rice

1 can cream of chicken or
  cream of mushroom soup
1 soup can water

Sprinkle the dry onion soup and the uncooked rice over the bottom of a covered baking pan. Place piece of chicken on the rice. Combine soup and water and pour over the chicken and rice. Cover and bake at 300 degrees for 1 hour and 15 minutes.

CHICKEN CASSEROLE

1 chicken or 4 large breasts
2 cups herb dressing mix
2 cups cornbread dressing mix
1 stick margarine, melted

1 small onion chopped
1 can cream of mushroom soup
1 soup can, 10 1/2 ounces of
  reserved chicken broth

Stew chicken until done, do not add salt. Pull off bones and set aside - saving broth. Stir together dressing mixes, onion, and melted margarine. Combine mushroom soup and chicken broth. In a greased dish put a layer of dressing crumbs, a layer of chicken, a layer of soup mixture and end with another layer of crumbs. Bake in a 350 degree preheated oven until brown. 45 minutes to 1 hour.

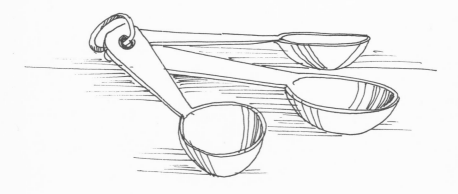

CHICKEN BREAST CASSEROLE

4 chicken breasts
1 package frozen chopped
  broccoli
1 can cream of chicken soup
Juice of 1 lemon

1/2 cup mayonnaise, not
  salad dressing
3/4 teaspoon curry powder
Cheese Ritz crackers

Broil chicken until tender, about 35 minutes. Strip meat off of bones, removing gristle while keeping large sections of the breast meat intact. Cook the broccoli. Mix soup, mayonnaise, lemon juice and curry powder. Combine mixture with chicken breasts. Add broccoli and pour into buttered casserole. Crush crackers and sprinkle crumbs over top. Cover casserole and bake at 350 degrees for about 35 minutes. Casserole may be prepared ahead and refrigerated until time for cooking. After refrigeration, allow a little extra time in oven. A double recipe fills a 1 1/2 quart casserole nicely. This casserole with a fruit salad is a nice luncheon menu.

CHICKEN CACCIATORE

1 10 ounce chicken breast
1 teaspoon salt
1/2 teaspoon pepper
Paprika
4 tablespoons instant minced
  onion flakes
1/2 cup sliced mushrooms
1/4 cup chopped celery

1/4 cup chopped pimientos
1 clove garlic, minced
1/8 teaspoon rosemary leaves
Pinch of allspice
2 cups tomato juice
1 tablespoon wine vinegar
1 tablespoon lemon juice

Sprinkle chicken with salt, pepper and paprika. Broil until done. Allow to cool and shred chicken by pulling apart into small pieces. Transfer chicken to baking dish. Combine onion, mushrooms, celery, pimiento, garlic, rosemary, allspice and tomato juice. Cook, uncovered over low heat, until tomato juice is reduced by half. Stir in lemon juice and vinegar. Pour sauce over chicken and bake at 325 degrees for 20 minutes.

77

CHICKEN BREAST BAKED IN WINE

4 whole chicken breasts split
4 tablespoons minced parsley
2 cloves garlic, pressed
1 1/2 cups Sherry wine

4 tablespoons slivered blanched
 almonds
1 can cream of chicken soup
1 can cream of mushroom soup

Mix soups together and add sherry and garlic. Place chicken in casserole, cover with soup mixture and sprinkle parsley and almonds on top. Cover and cook in oven 1 1/2 hours at 350 degrees.

CHICKEN IN WINE WITH SOUR CREAM GRAVY

4 to 6 chicken breasts
1/4 cup butter or margarine
Salt and pepper to taste
1 cup white wine
1/2 cup chopped celery

1 tablespoon dried onion
 flakes
1 tablespoon Brandy
1 cup sour cream

Melt butter in skillet and brown chicken breasts well. Combine remaining ingredients, except sour cream and pour over chicken. Cover and cook for 20 to 30 minutes or until chicken is tender. Remove chicken from skillet. Stir in sour cream and blend until gravy is smooth. Return chicken to skillet and keep warm until ready to serve. Can of cream of chicken soup may be substituted for sour cream if desired.

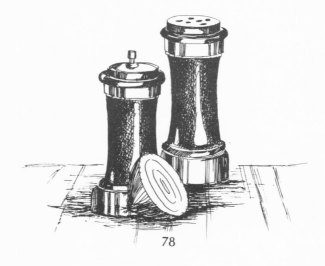

RICE AND CHICKEN CASSEROLE

2 chicken breast, halved
1 (10 1/2 ounce) can cream
   of mushroom soup
1 soup can milk
3/4 cup uncooked regular rice

1 (4 ounce) can mushroom stems
   and pieces
1 envelope dry onion soup mix

Heat oven to 350 degrees. Mix mushroom soup and milk and reserve 1/2 cup of the mixture. Mix remaining soup mixture, rice, mushrooms (with liquid) and half the onion soup mix. Pour into ungreased baking dish 11½x7½x1½ inches. Place chicken breast on top. Pour reserved soup mixture oven chicken breasts; sprinkle with remaining onion soup mix. Cover with aluminum foil; bake 1 hour. Uncover and bake 15 minutes.

Yield: 4 servings

LEMON PEPPER CHICKEN

1 - 2 1/2 to 3 pound frying
   chicken, cut up
1 1/2 to 2 teaspoons lemon
   pepper seasoning

1 1/2 to 2 teaspoons garlic salt
1 1/2 to 2 teaspoons oregano
1/4 cup fresh lemon juice
1/4 cup margarine, melted

Sprinkle oregano, garlic salt, and lemon pepper seasoning on both sides of chicken. Place in bowl and pour lemon juice over chicken. Cover and refrigerate several hours or overnight. Place chicken, skin side down, in bottom of broiler pan; brush with melted butter. Broil at 350 10 to 15 minutes or until golden brown. Turn; brush with butter. Broil 20-25 minutes or until done.

Yield: 6 servings

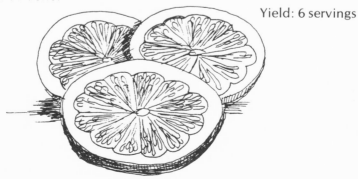

CHICKEN AND NOODLE CASSEROLE

3 or 4 pound chicken, boiled,
    skinned and boned
1 (8 ounce) package egg noodles
    cooked in chicken broth
1 can chicken soup

1 can cream of mushroom soup
1/2 pint sour cream
1 stick of margarine or butter
Cracker crumbs

Boil chicken. Bone and discard skin. Cook noodles in chicken broth and drain. Mix soups and sour cream together and heat. Combine with noodles. Pour in enough to cover the bottom of a shallow baking dish with noddle mixture. Arrange chicken on top and add remaining noodles. Top with cracker crumbs. Melt margarine and pour over casserole. Heat in oven until hot and bubbly.

CHICKEN NOODLE BAKE

3 to 4 cups cooked boned
    chicken
1 can cream celery soup
2 cups cooked noodles
    (4 ounces uncooked)

1/2 cup milk
1 cup peas
2 tablespoons diced pimiento
Buttered bread crumbs

Combine all ingredients except crumbs and blend well. Pour into a casserole, sprinkle with buttered crumbs, and bake at 375 degrees for 25 minutes.

Yield: 6-8 servings.

TETRAZZINI: TURKEY OR CHICKEN

1 1/2 cups cooked turkey
or chicken, cut in strips
3/4 cup cooked spaghetti
1 cup white sauce
1/4 teaspoon paprika
1/4 teaspoon mustard
Pepper to taste

Few drops onion juice
1/2 cup mushroom caps,
chopped
Butter or margarine
1/3 cup grated Parmesan
or Cheddar cheese
3/4 cup buttered bread crumbs

Saute mushrooms in butter and set aside. Make white sauce and add paprika, pepper, mustard, and onion juice. Bring sauce to a boil and add turkey, spaghetti and mushrooms. Pour into greased individual casseroles (or one large one.) Top with cheese and buttered crumbs. Bake at 425 degrees until the crumbs are brown.

CHICKEN LOAF

1 3/4 cup chopped cold
chicken
1/4 teaspoon celery salt
1 teaspoon parsley, chopped
fine

1 teaspoon lemon juice
Pepper to taste
1/4 cup thick white sauce
1/2 teaspoon salt
Few drops onion juice

Combine chicken, celery salt, parsley, lemon juice, salt and pepper. Fold in white sauce. Place in loaf pan and bake at 350 degrees for 45 minutes.

CHICKEN SPAGHETTI CASSEROLE

1 chicken
1/2 bunch celery, chopped
1 1/2 cups chopped onion
1/2 package spaghetti,
    broken in half

1 small can mushrooms
1/2 teaspoon chili powder
1/4 pound grated sharp cheese
1 can cream or mushroom soup

Cook chicken and remove meat from bones in large pieces. Cook celery and onion in chicken broth then drain and save broth. Cook spaghetti in half water and half chicken broth until tender, then drain. Heat mushroom soup, mushrooms and chili powder. Add celery and onions, spaghetti, chicken, and most of cheese. Mix all together, pour into baking dish and sprinkle remaining cheese on top. Cover and refrigerate a day or two. Bake 350 degrees for 1 hour.

CHICKEN SPAGHETTI

1-5 pound hen
2 small onions, chopped
1 large package spaghetti,
    cooked
Chicken broth

3 slices bacon
1 large green pepper, chopped
1/2 pound grated cheese
1 small can pimiento, chopped

Cook hen in salted water until tender. Remove from bones and dice. Chop and fry bacon. Add onion and pepper and cook until tender. Do not brown. Combine this with cooked spaghetti, chicken, cheese, pimiento and enough broth to moisten. Heat at 350 degrees until cheese melts.

Yield: 16-20 servings

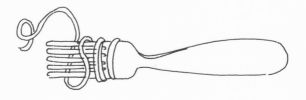

HOT CHICKEN SALAD

2 cups chopped chicken
1 cup cracker crumbs
2 cups finely chopped celery
2 cans cream of chicken soup
4 tablespoons grated onion

1 cup slivered almonds
1 cup mayonnaise
6 hard-boiled eggs, grated
Salt to taste
4 tablespoons lemon juice

Mix all ingredients together and put in buttered 8-inch glass baking dish. Add a few cracker crumbs and paprika on top. Bake at 350 degrees for 40-50 minutes. Make sure it is bubbly all over.

Yield: 8 servings

CHICKEN SALAD

2 cups chicken or turkey, chopped
1/2 cup chopped onions
1 cup finely chopped apples

1/2 cup chopped pickles
1 cup mayonnaise
1/2 cup finely chopped celery

Mix well and refrigerate until ready to use. Can be used for sandwiches or salad on lettuce.

SKILLET CHICKEN

1 - 3 pound fryer
Salt and pepper to taste
Paprika to taste
1 (4 ounce) can mushrooms
1/4 cup red wine

1 (8 ounce) can tomato sauce
1/4 teaspoon thyme
2 green peppers, cut
  in strips
1 medium onion, sliced

Cut chicken into serving pieces and sprinkle with salt, pepper and paprika. Drain mushrooms, reserving liquid. Then in a skillet, brown the chicken in a small amount of fat and remove from pan. Stir in wine, tomato sauce, mushroom liquid and thyme. Stir until well blended. Add chicken and mushrooms. Cover and simmer for 25 minutes.

COQ AU VIN

2 small broilers cut in
  half, lengthwise
1/4 cup unsweetened
  pineapple

1/4 teaspoon nutmeg
1 stick butter
1/4 cup dry white wine,
  Port or Sherry

Salt chicken and let stand for 1 hour, then pan broil gently in butter until lightly browned and reserve drippings. Place chicken in baking dish or electric skillet. Add pineapple, juice, wine, and nutmeg. Cover and simmer for 30 minutes at 300 degrees turning occasionally. (Add water if necessary). Add juices from skillet drippings, simmer and dilute with water to desired consistency, about 2 cups.

Yield: 4 servings

SWEET AND SOUR CHICKEN I

1 frying chicken, cut up
1/2 cup flour
1/2 cup vegetable shortening
1/2 cup white vinegar
1/2 cup brown sugar, firmly
  packed

1 1/2 teaspoon salt
1/4 teaspoon ginger
1/8 teaspoon pepper
1 medium orange, sliced
1 medium lemon, quartered

Dredge chicken in flour and brown in shortening over medium heat. Combine vinegar, sugar, salt, ginger and pepper and mix well. Pour over chicken, then add orange slices and lemon wedges. Reduce heat and simmer, covered, for 30 minutes or until tender.

SWEET AND SOUR CHICKEN II

2 1/2 cups cut-up cooked
  chicken
1 egg, slightly beaten
1/4 cup cornstarch
2 tablespoons shortening
1 (13 ounce) can pineapple
  chunks, drained (reserve
  syrup)
1/2 cup vinegar

1 medium green pepper, cut into
  1-inch squares
1/4 cup water
2 tablespoons cornstarch
1 teaspoon soy sauce
1 (16 ounce) can small
  carrots, drained
3 cups hot cooked rice
1/2 cup sugar

Toss chicken and egg until all pieces are coated. Sprinkle 1/4 cup cornstarch over chicken and toss again until all pieces are coated. Melt shortening in medium skillet. Add chicken pieces and cook over medium heat until brown. Remove chicken from skillet and set aside. Add enough water to pineapple syrup to measure 1 cup. Stir juice, vinegar, and sugar into skillet. Heat to boiling, stirring constantly. Stir in green pepper and bring to a boil. Reduce heat; cover and simmer 2 minutes. Blend water and 2 tablespoons cornstarch together. Stir into skillet and cook, stirring constantly until mixture thickens and boils. Boil and stir 1 minute. Stir in pineapple chunks, soy sauce, carrots and chicken; heat through.   Yield: 4 servings

INDIA CHICKEN CURRY

4 cups diced, cooked chicken
1/2 cup finely chopped onion
1/2 cup finely chopped celery
1/4 cup grease or oil
1/3 cup flour

2 cups chicken stock
1 cup tomato juice
1/2 teaspoon worcestershire
1 teaspoon curry powder
4 cups hot, cooked rice

Lightly brown onion and celery in hot fat. Add flour and blend. Add stock and cook until thick, stirring constantly. Add tomato juice, worcestershire sauce, seasonings and chicken. Heat thoroughly. Serve over cooked rice or make ring mold of rice and fill center with curry mixture.

Yield: 10 servings

CHICKEN A LA KING CHOW MEIN

1 (10 1/2 ounce) can
  cream of celery soup
1 cup cooked chicken,
1 (4 ounce) can mushroom
  stems and pieces, drained

1 tablespoon chopped pimiento
1 teaspoon parsley flakes
Salt and pepper
Chow mein noodles, rice or toast

Heat soup. Stir in remaining ingredients except chow mein noodles. Heat through and serve over chow mein noodles, rice or toast.

Yield: 3 or 4 servings

EXOTIC MANDARIN CHICKEN

3 large whole chicken breasts
1/3 cup flour
Salt and pepper to taste
1/4 cup cooking oil
1/2 cup sliced onion
3/4 cup diagonally sliced
  celery
1 clove of garlic
1 can cream of mushroom soup
1/4 cup chicken broth

1 (5 ounce) can sliced mushrooms,
  drained
1 (6 ounce) can water chestnuts,
  drained
1 (7 ounce) package frozen pea pods,
  thawed
1 (11 ounce) can mandarin oranges,
  drained

Cut chicken breasts in half. Coat chicken with flour; sprinkle with salt and pepper. Brown in hot oil in skillet. Remove chicken from skillet. Add the onion, celery and garlic; cook until tender. Remove garlic. Blend in soup, broth, mushrooms, water chestnuts, pea pods and mandarin oranges. Return chicken to skillet until serving time.

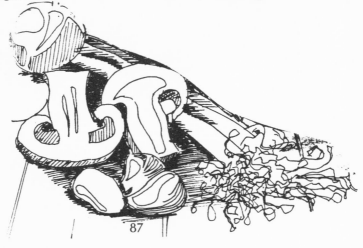

BRAISED CHICKEN WINGS

1/4 cup soy sauce
1/2 cup water
2 tablespoons brown sugar
1/4 cup sherry
1 teaspoon dry mustard

2 green onions cut in
  1-inch pieces
10 chicken wings,
  separated at joints

Combine all ingredients in medium-size saucepan. Cover and heat to boiling, then reduce heat and simmer 30 minutes. Uncover and simmer 15 minutes longer, basting frequently. Serve hot or cold.

Yield: 6 servings

BARBECUED CHICKEN I

1 - 2 1/2 to 3 pound fryer,
  quartered
2 tablespoons salt
1/4 cup brown sugar
2 tablespoons sugar
1 teaspoon worcestershire

2 teaspoons pepper
3 tablespoons cayenne pepper
3 cups vinegar
3 tablespoons catsup
2 tablespoons red hot sauce

Place chicken in shallow baking pan. Combine salt, sugars and peppers. Add worcestershire sauce, vinegar, catsup and hot sauce. Mix well and pour over chicken. Bake 1 1/2 hours or until chicken is tender.

Yield: 4 servings

BARBECUED CHICKEN II

1 - 3 to 4 pound fryer
1/2 cup diced celery
3/4 cup chopped onion
3/4 cup vegetable shortening
1/2 cup catsup
1 teaspoon salt

1/8 teaspoon red pepper
1 cup water
2 teaspoons lemon juice
1 1/2 tablespoons prepared
   mustard

Cut chicken into quarters or pieces and place on a greased rack in a greased shallow pan. Brown onion and celery in shortening. Add remaining ingredients and simmer for 15 minutes covered. Pour 1/4 of mixture over chicken and bake in a 350 degree oven for 1 1/2 hours. Baste every 20 to 25 minutes with 1/4 of sauce. Turn chicken over after 45 minutes.

BARBEQUE CHICKEN SANDWICHES

1 chicken, boiled-skinned, boned, and chopped

SAUCE

1 can tomato juice
1 onion, chopped
1 tablespoon mustard
1 teaspoon chili powder

1/4 cup vinegar
Dash of garlic powder
Pinch of oregano
Sweeten to taste

Combine sauce ingredients, mix well. Mix chicken and as much sauce as you like. Simmer. Serve on bread or buns.

BARBECUED BROILED CHICKEN

1 - 2 1/2 pound young
  chicken
1 teaspoon salt
1/2 teaspoon black pepper
1 tablespoon paprika
Dash of cayenne
1/4 teaspoon dry (or 1
  teaspoon prepared mustard)
1 tablespoon sugar
1/3 cup water
2 tablespoons worcestershire

1/3 cup vinegar or lemon
  juice
Bottled barbecue sauce
  or steak sauce
1/4 cup margarine
1/2 clove garlic or 1/2
  teaspoon garlic salt
1/2 cup catsup, optional
1 onion, finely chopped
  optional

Blend salt, pepper, paprika, cayenne, mustard and sugar. Add water and heat to boiling. Remove from heat and add vinegar, or lemon juice, worcestershire, bottled barbecue or steak sauce, butter, garlic, catsup and onion. Blend evenly. Quarter chicken as for broiling. Brush with melted butter and place skin side down directly on broiler pan, no rack. Place in oven 5-7 inches from heat source setting control at 500-550, or broil. Watch carefully and turn when lightly brown. When both sides have been browned begin spooning barbecue sauce over chicken and keep turning and basting until chicken is well browned. Do not burn. Now reset oven to a lower temperature 350 degrees and cook until very tender. The time will vary from 1 hour to 1 1/2 hours depending on size of chicken. It is possible to brown on both sides and cook at 300 from 1 1/2 to 2 1/2 hours, eliminating much of the watching.

Yield: 4 servings

ROAST CHICKEN AND STUFFING

1 fryer, 3 to 4
  pounds
1/2 onion, minced
1 cup diced celery
4 tablespoons fat
1 teaspoon salt
1/4 teaspoon pepper

4 cups bread crumbs,
  firmly packed
1/2 teaspoon poultry,
  seasoning
1/2 to 1 cup broth, water
  or milk

Cook onion and celery in fat over low heat, stirring occasionally until onion is soft but not browned. Meanwhile, blend seasonings with bread crumbs. Add onion, celery and fat. Blend. Pour broth over crumbs, stirring lightly. Add more seasoning if desired. After rubbing chicken cavity with 1/2 teaspoon salt, stuff body cavities lightly. Roast bird on rack on open pan in a 350 degree oven for about 2 hours. Baste occasionally. Chicken is done when thickest part of the drumstick feels soft when pressed and when the juice in the leg joint show no trace of pink, when pierced by a fork.

Yield: 4 servings

CHICKEN AND DRESSING

1 4-5 pound hen
1 large onion, chopped
2 cups chopped celery
1 cup water
Chicken stock
2 tablespoons salt

3 tablespoons pepper
Sage to taste
1 large pan of corn bread,
  crumbled
3 cups toasted white
  bread cubes

Cook hen in boiling water until tender. Preheat oven to 350 degrees. Combine onion, celery, and 1 cup water. Cook until tender. Combine other ingredients, adding enough chicken stock to moisten. Put mixture in baking dish. Bake about 1 hour.

Yield: 6 to 8 servings

HERBED TURKEY CASSEROLE

2 cups diced cooked turkey
2 cups elbow macaroni
cooked and drained
1 can cream of mushroom soup
1 1/2 cups milk
2 tablespoons instant
minced onions
1 teaspoon salt

1/2 teaspoon poultry
seasoning
1/2 teaspoon leaf basil,
crumbled
Dash of pepper
1/4 cup packaged bread crumbs
1 tablespoon butter, melted

Combine macaroni, turkey, soup, milk, onion, and seasonings in a large bowl. Mix well. Turn into buttered 2-quart casserole. Cover and bake at 350 degrees for 25 minutes or until mixture is heated through. Mix bread crumbs with melted butter or margarine and spread evenly over casserole. Place under broiler until crumbs are lightly browned.

Yield: 5 to 6 servings

TURKEY A LA KING

3 tablespoons butter
2 tablespoons chopped green
pepper
2 tablespoons chopped
pimiento
3 tablespoons flour
1 can mushroom soup

1/4 teaspoon salt
1 tablespoon sweet relish
2 cups diced, cooked turkey
2 egg yolks
Patty shells or toast

Melt butter in saucepan and add green pepper and pimiento Cook slowly until slightly brown. Add flour and blend well. Add mushroom soup, salt and stir until thick. Add relish, turkey and heat thoroughly. Add the well-beaten egg yolks and continue cooking for only 2 or 3 minutes more. Serve in patty shells or on toast.

Yield: 4 servings

TURKEY ROAST

4 pound rolled turkey roast
1 cup white wine or
   apple juice
1/2 teaspoon salt
1/8 teaspoon pepper

1/8 teaspoon sage
1/8 teaspoon thyme
1/4 cup water
2 tablespoons flour

Bake turkey roast as directed on package except--before roasting, mix wine, salt, pepper, sage and thyme and pour over roast; baste occasionally.

Remove roast from pan; keep warm. Skim fat from broth. Measure broth; return 1 cup to roasting pan. In covered jar, shake water and flour and stir slowly into broth. Heat to boiling, stirring constantly. Boil and stir 1 minute.

Yield: 8 servings

TURKEY LEFTOVERS

3 cups diced, cooked turkey
4 tablespoons butter, divided
1/4 cup chopped onion
1 (3 ounce) can mushroom
   crowns and liquid
5 tablespoons flour
3 cups water
1 teaspoon salt

3/4 cup instant nonfat
   dry milk powder
1/4 teaspoon pepper
1/2 teaspoon paprika
2 tablespoons Sherry,
optional
1/2 cup blanched almonds
   split or slivered

Saute onions until golden brown in two tablespoons butter. Add mushrooms and liquid. Cook until liquid evaporates. Stir in turkey. Place water in a deep one-quart bowl. Sprinkle the nonfat dry milk powder, flour and seasonings over surface. Beat with rotary beater just until blended. Pour over turkey mixture. Cook over medium heat, stirring constantly, until mixture thickens and comes to a boil. Add Sherry. Brown almonds in remaining butter. Serve the turkey amandine over rice, toast rounds, or in timbales. Sprinkle top with browned almonds.

ROAST DUCK

1 duck (Long Island or wild)
1 cup orange juice
1/2 cup cooking Sherry

1 teaspoon salt
1 whole orange
   (preferably seedless)

Truss and place breast side down in covered pan. Combine orange juice, Sherry and salt; pour over duck. Bake 35 minutes per pound at 350 degrees; basting every 10 minutes. Garnish with orange slices.

CHICKEN LIVER CASSEROLE

8 ounces chicken livers
1 can cream of chicken soup
Minced onions
1 1/2 cups cooked rice

1/3 cup milk
Basil
Parsley
Butter

Lightly brown livers in butter; add minced onions. Mix chicken soup with milk and add basil, parsley and rice. Stir together with livers and bake at 375 degrees for 30 minutes.

Seafood

SEAFOOD

SEAFOOD

OYSTER SOUFFLE

1 pint oysters	1 teaspoon salt
3 tablespoons butter	1/8 teaspoon pepper
3 tablespoons flour	Dash of nutmeg
1 cup milk	3 eggs, separated

Drain and chop oysters. Melt butter and blend in flour, add milk, stirring constantly. Cook 3 minutes. Add oysters, seasonings, and beaten egg yolks. Beat egg whites until stiff, fold into oyster mixture. Pour into buttered casserole and bake in moderate oven 350 degrees about 30 minutes or until brown.

Yield: 6 servings

ESCALLOPED OYSTERS

1 pint standard oysters
2 envelopes saltine crackers,
  (1/2 pound) can use less
1/2 to 3/4 stick of margarine
1 egg

Chicken broth or can of
  concentrated chicken soup
  diluted with milk plus
1 bouillion cube

Break about 1/3 of crackers into bottom of large casserole. Pour in half the oysters and mix thoroughly with fingers. Break more crackers in casserole and pour in rest of oysters. Mix lightly and top with rest of broken crackers. Moisten crackers until soggy with hot, rich chicken broth. Be sure the broth is boiling when poured over oysters and crackers. Dot with margarine. Cook until lightly browned. Beat egg thoroughly and pour over top. Brown until crusty. Serve piping hot.

Yield: 4 to 6 servings

    I always cook my hens with celery and onions. This makes the broth very tasty. If you don't have chicken broth on hand use a can of concentrated chicken soup, diluted with milk and add a chicken boullion cube.

OYSTER STEW

1 quart oysters, drained
4 cups light cream
2 cups milk
Paprika

1/4 cup butter or margarine
1/2 teaspoon salt
Dash of Pepper
1/2 teaspoon Worcestershire

Combine all ingredients except paprika in heavy saucepan. Bring to low boil. Cook until edges of oysters begin to curl. Remove from heat. Serve immediately with dash of paprika.

Yield: 6 servings.

BOILED SHRIMP

2 pounds raw, shrimp, fresh   5 cups water
   or frozen   2 tablespoons salt

Thaw shrimp if frozen. Peel and devein shrimp. Rinse shrimp thoroughly and drain. Add salt to water and bring to a boil. Add shrimp and reduce heat. Cover and simmer 3 to 4 minutes or until the largest shrimp is opaque in the center when tested by cutting in half. (Cooking time will vary according to size of shrimp. Jumbo shrimp will require a little longer cooking time.) Drain shrimp. Rinse thoroughly for 1 to 2 minutes under cold running water. Serve warm or cold with Chilli Sauce. Yields approximately one pound cooked, peeled, deveined shrimp.

FRENCH FRIED SHRIMP

1 1/2 pounds raw shrimp   1/2 cup plain flour
   peeled and deveined   1/2 cup dry bread crumbs
   (fresh or frozen)   1/2 teaspoon paprika
2 eggs, beaten   Oil for deep frying
1 teaspoon salt   Chilli or Tartar Sauce

Thaw shrimp if frozen. Combine eggs and salt. Combine flour, bread crumbs and paprika. Dip each shrimp in egg, then roll in crumb mixture. Fry in a basket in deep fat, 350 degrees, for 2 to 3 minutes or until golden brown. Drain on absorbent paper. Serve with Chilli or Tartar Sauce.

Yield: 6 servings.

IMPERIAL SEAFOOD CASSEROLE

1 pound frozen crabmeat
1/2 cup chopped onions
1 cup sliced celery
2 tablespoons margarine or
  butter
1 can cream of mushroom soup
1 teaspoon poultry seasoning

1 (7 ounce) can pimiento,
  chopped
3 cups cooked rice
Salt and pepper to taste
1 (5 ounce) package French
  fried onion rings

Thaw crabmeat and cut into 1 inch chunks. Saute onions and celery in butter until tender-crisp. Add soup, crabmeat, pimiento, rice and seasonings. Turn into a greased 2 quart casserole. Top with onion rings and bake in a preheated 350 degree oven for 25 minutes.

Yield: 6 servings

SEAFOOD COQUILLIES

1 (12 ounce) package frozen
  scallops, thawed, drained
  and quartered
1 (10 ounce) package, frozen
  cooked shrimp, thawed
  and drained
1 (6 ounce) can sliced
  mushrooms, drained

2 cans cream of shrimp
  soup
1 tablespoon grated lemon
  peel
1 tablespoon chopped chives
Grated Parmesan cheese
  or French fried onion rings

Mix thoroughly all ingredients except cheese. Place about 1 cup of mixture in each of 5 or 6 baking shells or individual casseroles. Place shells on baking sheet. Bake 15 minutes at 400 degrees. Remove from oven, top shells with cheese or onion rings and bake 2 to 3 minutes longer.

DEVILED CRAB

4 cups crabmeat frozen
1 cup milk
1 1/2 cups cracker crumbs,
  divided
3 tablespoons minced parsley
1 1/2 tablespoon grated onion
3/4 teaspoon salt
1/2 cup butter

Dash of pepper
Dash of tabasco sauce
3 tablespoons Worcestershire
1 tablespoon prepared mustard
1 green pepper, finely
  chopped
1 pimiento, finely chopped
2 hard-cooked eggs, grated

In saucepan combine all ingredients except crabmeat and 1/2 cup cracker crumbs. Cook over medium heat for about 10 minutes. Add crabmeat and cook about 5 minutes more. Lightly butter 8 individual crab shells or 2 quart casserole dish. Pour crab mixture into casserole and top with remaining crumbs. Brown in oven.

Yield: 8 servings

FRIED CATFISH

1 tablespoon salt
1 tablespoon pepper
1 cup all-purpose flour
1 quart cooking oil

1 cup cornmeal
18 fresh Tennessee River catfish,
Weighing about 3/4 pound each

Combine flour, cornmeal, salt and pepper in heavy bag. Wash fish. While still wet, shake each one in bag. Pour oil to depth of 1 inch in heavy skillet. Heat to 370 degrees. Cook fish 2 or 3 at a time until crisp on both sides, turning once during cooking. Add more oil as needed. Keep warm in 200 degree oven on baking sheet lined with brown paper.

Yield: 6 to 8 servings

SALMON LOAF

1 (16 ounce) can salmon
1/2 cup bread crumbs
1/8 teaspoon salt
1/8 teaspoon pepper
2 eggs, separated

1 tablespoon lemon juice
1 cup hot milk
2 tablespoons butter, melted
Chopped onions or parsley
  may be added

Combine salmon, crumbs, salt and pepper, egg yolks, lemon juice, milk and butter. Beat egg whites and fold into mixture. Bake in buttered pan at 350 degrees for 1 hour.

BAKED RED SNAPPER

2 pounds red snapper steaks,
  cut 1/3 inch thick
Salt and pepper
Parsley sprigs

1 tablespoon grated lemon rind
Paprika
1/3 cup butter or margarine,
  melted

Preheat oven to 400 degrees. Place fish in a greased oblong baking dish. Sprinkle with salt, pepper, lemon rind, and paprika. Cover dish with aluminum foil or lid. Bake fish steaks about 15 minutes. Check to see if fish is done, if so, remove foil. Pour on melted butter. Return to oven for 2 minutes. Garnish with parsley.

FILET OF SOLE

6 pieces filet of sole
  (about 2 pounds)
1 tablespoon lemon juice
3/4 teaspoon salt
1/4 teaspoon pepper
6 thin slices onion
1 medium-size tomato, peeled
  and cut in thin wedges

1/2 cup chopped green pepper
3 tablespoons chopped parsley
2 tablespoons olive or
  pure vegetable oil
1/3 cup sliced, stuffed olives
1 tablespoon flour
1 tablespoon cold water

Preheat oven to 350 degrees. Place filets in buttered, shallow baking dish. Drizzle lemon juice over fish; sprinkle with salt and pepper. Place 1 onion slice on each filet. Combine tomato, green pepper, parsley, oil, and olives; spoon over fish. Bake, covered, 25 minutes or until fish flakes easily. Remove fish to heated platter; keep warm. Blend flour to smooth paste with cold water and stir into hot fish stock in baking dish. Cook, stirring constantly, until sauce thickens. Serve with hot filets.

Yield: 6 servings.

CHEESY TUNA CASSEROLE

1 3/4 cup skim milk
2 teaspoons cornstarch
1 teaspoon salt
1/2 teaspoon black pepper
1 teaspoon chopped onions
   instant or fresh

2 ounces cheese
7 ounces tuna, drained
1 cup cooked macaroni
8 ounce green peas
Paprika

In medium saucepan make a white sauce by combining cornstarch, salt and pepper and enough milk to make a paste. Then slowly stir in remaining milk. Add onions and cook over medium heat stirring constantly until mixture thickens. Add cheese to sauce and heat until cheese melts. Remove from heat and stir in macaroni, peas and tuna. Pour mixture into small shallow baking dish and sprinkle lightly with paprika. Bake at 425 degrees approximately 30 minutes or until brown and bubbly.

Yield 2 to 3 servings.

TUNA SUPREME

1 (6 1/2 ounce) can tuna
   drained, flaked
1 (7 1/4 ounce) package
   macaroni and cheese dinner
1/2 cup milk
1/4 teaspoon celery salt

1 (2 1/2 ounce) jar sliced
   mushrooms, drained
1/2 cup sour cream
1 (8 ounce) can peas and
   carrots, drained
1/4 cup chopped onion

Prepare macaroni and cheese dinner as directed on package using 1/2 cup milk. Add remaining ingredients and mix well. Pour into 1 1/2 quart casserole. Cover and bake at 350 degrees, 20 minutes.

Yield: 4 servings.

Vegetables

VEGETABLES

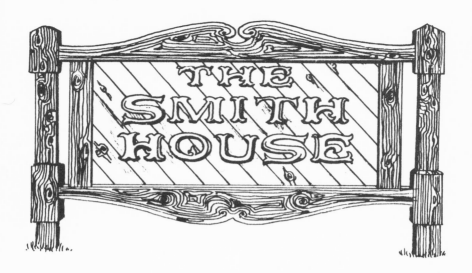

VEGETABLES

CHESTNUT SOUFFLE

1 pound chestnuts	3 eggs, separated
Pinch of salt	1 teaspoon vanilla
Milk	Confectioner's sugar
1/2 cup sugar	Brandy, optional
1/3 cup heavy cream	

Shell and peel chestnuts. Put them in a saucepan with enough milk to cover and bring just to a boil. Simmer for about 30 minutes or until chestnuts are soft. Drain and force chestnuts through a fine sieve or puree them in a blender.

In a saucepan combine the puree with sugar and cream. Cook slowly, stirring constantly, until mixture is smooth and thick. Remove from heat and stir in egg yolks, vanilla and brandy, if desired. Fold in stiffly beaten egg whites; and put souffle in buttered 1-1/2 quart souffle dish. Bake at 350 degrees for 30 - 40 minutes or until souffle is firm. Sprinkle with confectioners sugar and serve at once.

ASPARAGUS CASSEROLE

1 can asparagus
1 cup crushed Ritz crakers
3 hard boiled eggs
Butter or margarine

1 can cream of mushroom soup
Black pepper, to taste
Grated cheese

Drain asparagus. Reserve liquid. Alternate layers of asparagus, crushed crackers, and sliced hard boiled eggs. Pour asparagus liquid over, dot with butter, and season with black pepper. Top with mushroom soup. Sprinkle with grated cheese. Bake 350 degrees until bubbly.

ASPARAGUS-PEA CASSEROLE

1 cup asparagus tips,
  drained
2 cups canned sweet peas,
  drained
2 hard boiled eggs, sliced
2 tablespoons grated cheese

2 tablespoons butter
1 cup mushroom soup
1/2 cup milk
1/2 cup cracker crumbs
1/2 cup sliced almonds

Grease casserole with part of the butter. Layer asparagus, peas, egg slices, and cheese. Mix soup and milk. Pour over casserole. Top with cracker crumbs and almonds. Dot with remaining butter. Bake 425 degrees for 30 minutes.

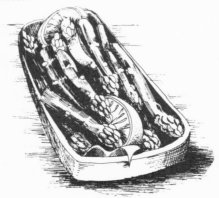

BROCCOLI CASSEROLE

2 (10 ounce) packages frozen
  broccoli, chopped
1/4 onion, grated

1/2 cup grated cheese
1 cup mayonnaise
2 eggs, beaten

Mix all ingredients and put in a casserole dish, sprinkle with bread crumbs. Bake for 30 minutes at 350 degrees.

EASY BROCCOLI CASSEROLE

2 (10 ounce) packages frozen
  chopped broccoli
2 (5 ounce) cans water chestnuts
2 cans cream of chicken soup

2 tablespoons dry bread
  crumbs
1/4 cup Parmesan cheese,
  grated
2 tablespoons butter, melted

In ungreased 2-quart casserole place broccoli and thinly sliced water chestnuts. Pour soup over casserole. Top with mixture of bread crumbs, cheese, and melted butter. Bake uncovered 350 degrees for 1 hour.

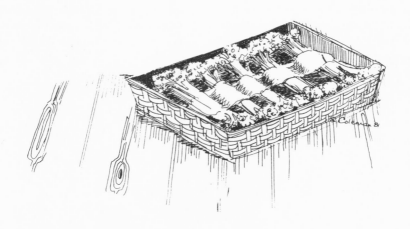

BROCCOLI AND RICE CASSEROLE

2 packages frozen broccoli
1 can cream of mushroom soup
1 cup cooked rice, cooled
1 onion, finely chopped
1/2 stick margarine

1/4 cup water
1/2 cup milk
1/2 cup cheese spread (or
  grated cheese)

Cook broccoli according to package directions; drain well, cool and chop. Saute onion in margarine. Mix broccoli, rice, water, milk, cheese, and onion. Bake in greased casserole at 350 degrees for 30 minutes.

BROCCOLI POLONAISE

2 (10 ounce) packages
  frozen broccoli
1/2 cup butter or margarine
2 tablespoons chopped parsley

1/2 cup packaged bread
  crumbs
2 hard-cooked eggs,
  finely chopped

Cook broccoli according to package directions. Drain. Arrange on serving dish. In a small skillet lightly brown bread crumbs in the melted butter. Sprinkle broccoli with eggs and parsley. Top with buttered bread crumbs.   Yield: 6 servings

GREEN BEAN CASSEROLE

2 cans French Style
  green beans
1 can mushroom soup

1 can French fried
  onion rings
1/2 can milk (large)

Drain beans and put 1 can in casserole dish. Sprinkle half of onions over beans. Combine soup and milk and pour half over green beans. Repeat layers and bake at 350 degrees until bubbling and onion rings look toasted. About 20 to 30 minutes.

BAKED BEANS

1 pound (2 cups) dry
  navy beans
1 1/2 quarts cold water
1 teaspoon salt
1/2 cup brown sugar

1 teaspoon salt
1 teaspoon dry mustard
1/4 cup molasses
1/4 pound salt pork
1 medium onion, sliced

Rinse beans and add to **cold** water. Bring to a full boil, lower heat and simmer for 2 minutes. Cover, remove from heat and let stand for one hour.

Add salt to soaking beans. Cover and simmer 1 hour, or until tender. Drain, reserving liquid. Combine 3/4 cup of bean liquid with sugar, salt, mustard, and molasses. Cut salt pork in half; score one half, set aside. Grind or thinly slice remainder.

In 2-quart bean pot or casserole, alternate layers of beans, onion, ground salt pork, and sugar mixture. Repeat layers. Top with scored salt pork. Cover. Bake in slow oven (300) for 5 to 7 hours, adding more liquid if needed.

CABBAGE CASSEROLE

1 large cabbage
1 can cream chicken soup
1 can cream of mushroom soup

1/2 cup crisp bacon, crumbled
Cheddar cheese

Slice cabbage. Cover with water salted to taste and steam until tender. Drain. Alternate a layer of cabbage with chicken soup with a layer of cabbage with mushroom soup until all the cabbage is used. Sprinkle with crumbled bacon. Top with grated cheese. Bake 425 degrees until casserole begins to bubble.

ORANGE-GINGER CARROTS

5 medium carrots
1 teaspoon cornstarch
1/4 teaspoon ginger
2 tablespoons margarine

1 tablespoon sugar
1/4 teaspoon salt
1/4 cup orange juice

Slice carrots about 1 inch thick. Cook, covered, in boiling salted water until barely tender, about 20 minutes. Drain. Combine sugar, cornstarch, salt, and ginger in small saucepan. Add orange juice, stirring constantly over medium heat until mixture thickens and bubbles. Boil 1 minute. Stir in butter. Pour over hot carrots. Toss to coat evenly.

CORN PUDDING CASSEROLE

1 (16 ounce) can
  cream-style corn
1/4 cup sweet bell peppers,
  finely chopped
1 cup milk

Salt and pepper to taste
2 eggs, well beaten
1/2 stick butter
1/4 cup onions, finely
  chopped

Mix corn, peppers, onions, eggs, butter, and milk. Salt and pepper to taste. Pour into casserole. Bake at 400 degrees for 35 - 40 minutes.

CORN CASSEROLE

1 (16 ounce) can of cream
  style corn
1 tablespoon butter
1/2 cup chopped sweet peppers

2 tablespoons chopped pimientos
1 egg
1 (3 1/2 ounce) can of French
  fried onions

Saute peppers in butter until soft. Add corn, egg, pimiento, and half of the can of onions, crushed fine. Blend all together well. Pour into a 1 1/2 quart greased casserole dish. Bake at 350 degrees for 25 to 30 minutes. Remove from oven. Put remaining onions, finely crushed, on top of casserole and bake for 5 to 10 minutes.

CORN CHOWDER

3 tablespoons diced salt pork
1/2 cup chopped onion
2 cups diced potatoes
2 cups boiling water
2 cans (1 lb. each) cream-
    style corn
1 quart milk

2 teaspoons salt
1/4 teaspoon pepper
1/4 teaspoon leaf rosemary,
    crumbled
1/4 cup diced pimiento
1/4 cup shredded Cheddar cheese
2 tablespoons minced parsley

Brown salt pork in large kettle or Dutch oven; remove browned bits; reserve. Add onion to drippings in kettle; saute until soft, do not brown. Add potatoes and water and simmer about 20 minutes or until potatoes are tender. Add corn, milk, salt, pepper, rosemary, pimiento, and browned pork bits. Heat until steaming hot. Sprinkle with cheese and parsley.

GRITS CASSEROLE DISH

1 1/2 cups left-over grits
1/2 cup grated cheese
1 egg, beaten

1 cup milk
1 tablespoon butter or margarine
Salt to taste

Mix grits with cheese, add beaten egg, milk and margarine. Salt to taste. Place in casserole and bake for 15 minutes at 350 degrees.

FRIED ONION RINGS
(Eggplant, Cauliflower, or Shrimp)

2/3 cup evaporated milk
1 egg, slightly beaten
1 tablespoon vegetable oil

1 cup sifted self-rising
  flour
Onion rings, 1/4 inch thick

Combine milk, egg and oil; stir in flour, mixing well. Allow batter to stand 15 minutes. Dip onions into batter. On temperature controlled burner set at 375, fry rings in deep fat until golden; drain on paper towels. Srinkle with salt.

FRENCH FRIED EGGPLANT

1 medium eggplant
1 cup sifted all-purpose
  flour
1/2 teaspoon salt

1 slightly beaten egg
1 cup milk
1 tablespoon salad oil
Parmesan cheese

Peel eggplant and cut lengthwise into 1/2 inch slices. Then cut each slice into 1/2 inch finger strips. Mix 1 cup sifted all-purpose flour with 1/2 teaspoon salt. Combine 1 slightly beaten egg, 1 cup milk, and 1 tablespoon salad oil; add gradually to flour mixture. Beat till smooth. Dip eggplants in batter, drain well. Fry in deep hot oil at 375 degrees for 2 to 5 minutes. Drain on paper towels. Sprinkle with salt and Parmesan cheese. Serve hot.

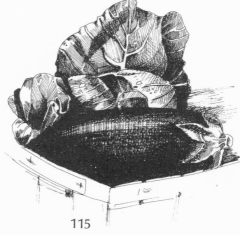

EGGPLANT CASSEROLE I

1 eggplant, pared and
cut in cubes
6 medium tomatoes, sliced
1/2 teaspoon pepper
1 large onion, diced

1 green pepper, diced
1/3 cup olive oil
2 teaspoon salt
1 teaspoon oregano

Brown eggplant, onions, and green pepper in oil. Stir in seasoning. Alternate layers of eggplant mixture with tomatoes in 1 1/2 quart casserole. Bake 40 minutes at 400 degrees.

EGGPLANT CASSEROLE II

1 medium eggplant
2 tablespoons butter
1 medium onion, chopped
2 eggs, beaten
1/2 cup milk

1 cup dry bread or
cracker crumbs
1/2 cup buttered bread crumbs
or cracker crumbs
1/2 cup grated cheddar cheese

Pare eggplant and cut into 1 inch cubes. Cook in boiling salted water until just tender. Drain and cool. In a small pan, saute onion in butter until golden brown. Combine eggplant, sauted onion, eggs, milk, and dry crumbs. Mix well. Place in greased quart casserole. Top with buttered crumbs and cheese. Bake at 350 for 30 minutes.

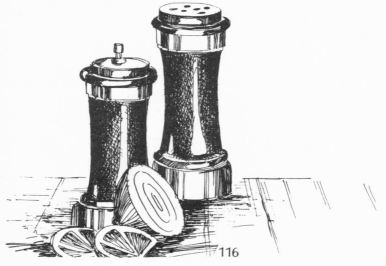

EGGPLANT PARMIGIANA

1 large eggplant, peeled and
  cut in 1/2 inch thick slices
1 teaspoon salt
1/2 cup olive oil
1/2 cup chopped onion
1 clove of garlic, chopped
1 (17 ounce) can Italian
  tomatoes, undrained
1/2 teaspoon oregano,
  crumbled

1/2 teaspoon basil, crumbled
1 teaspoon salt
1/4 teaspoon pepper
2 eggs
3 tablespoons flour
3/4 cup grated Parmesan
  cheese
8 ounces Mozzarella
  cheese, sliced

Sprinkle eggplant slices with 1 teaspoon salt. Let stand 30 minutes to draw out excess moisture; pat dry with paper towel. Heat 2 tablespoons olive oil in saucepan. Saute onion and garlic 5 minutes. Add tomatoes, basil, oregano, 1 teaspoon salt, and pepper. Cover and simmer 20 minutes.

Combine eggs and flour in a small bowl. Beat with rotary beater until smooth. Dip eggplant slices in egg mixture and drain slightly. Saute in hot oil on both sides; using 2 tablespoons oil at a time. Place a single layer of eggplant in shallow 2-quart baking dish. Cover with half the tomato sauce, half the Parmesan cheese, and half the Mozzarella. Repeat a second layer of eggplant, sauce, and Mozzarella. Sprinkle with remaining Parmesan. Bake in a preheated 350 degree oven for 25 minutes or until thoroughly heated.

Yield: 8 servings

SQUASH OR EGGPLANT CASSEROLE

1 eggplant or 4 cups
  cooked squash
2 eggs
1/3 cup chopped onion
1 cup toasted bread or
  cracker crumbs

1 can mushroom soup
1 tablespoon sugar
1 cup grated cheese
1/2 stick butter or margarine
  melted

Cook eggplant or squash in salted water until tender. Drain. Mix with soup, eggs, sugar. Put a layer of this mixture in casserole, then a layer of onions, cheese and bread crumbs. Repeat until all is used. Pour 1/2 stick melted butter over top. Sprinkle with cracker crumbs and bake 350 degrees for 30 minutes.

SQUASH AND APPLE BAKE

2-pound butternut or
  buttercup squash
1/2 cup brown sugar, packed
1/4 cup butter or margarine,
  melted

1 tablespoon flour
1 teaspoon salt
1/2 teaspoon mace
2 baking apples, cored and
  cut into 1/2 inch slices

Cut each squash in half and remove seed and fibers. Pare squash and cut into 1/2 inch slices. Stir together brown sugar, butter, flour, salt and mace. In an ungreased baking dish (11½x7½x1½ inches) place squash then the apples. Top with sugar mixture. Cover with foil. Bake at 350 degrees for 50-60 minutes, or until squash is tender.   Yield: 6 servings.

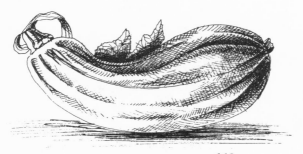

SQUASH CASSEROLE I

1 pound squash, cooked,
   mashed
1/4 cup mayonnaise
1 teaspoon sugar
1/4 cup chopped onion

1/2 cup crumbled crackers,
   divided
1/4 cup grated cheese
1 egg, beaten
Salt and pepper to taste

Mix squash, mayonnaise, sugar, onions, 1/4 cup crackers, and beaten egg. Put into baking dish. Top with remaining crackers and cheese. Cover and bake 350 degrees 25-30 minutes.

SQUASH CASSEROLE II

3 pounds of squash
2 medium onions, chopped
2 medium carrots, grated
1 cup sour cream

2 cans cream of chicken soup
1 package herb-seasoned dressing
   mix
1 stick butter or margarine

Cook squash, onions, and carrots in salted water until tender. Drain and add sour cream and soup. Mix dressing with butter. Alternate layers of the squash mixture with the buttered crumbs. End with crumbs on top. Bake at 350 degrees for 30 minutes.

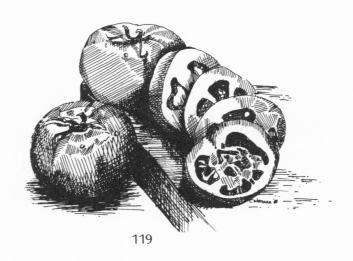

GLAZED BUTTERNUT SQUASH

1 (2 pound) butternut squash   1/4 teaspoon salt
1/2 teaspoon cinnamon   1/4 teaspoon nutmeg or ginger
1/2 cup brown sugar,   3 tablespoons butter, melted
    firmly packed

Peel, seed and slice squash. This needs to be cooked on a rack in a pan with a tight fitting cover. Place on rack and add enough water to cover bottom of pan. Cover and steam until squash is nearly tender, approximately 12 to 15 minutes. Drain well. Arrange the squash in one or two layers in a greased shallow baking dish. Mix sugar, spices and salt and sprinkle over the squash. Dribble melted butter over top. Bake at 400 degrees until the squash is tender and somewhat glazed, about 15 to 20 minutes. For a deeper glaze, broil a few minutes.

TURNIP GREENS

Turnip greens should be thoroughly washed to be free of grit. Remove any objectionable part of tough stem. For 1/2 peck of greens use just enough water to cover 1/4 lb. seasoning meat. Bring meat and water to a boil. Add greens and bring to a hard boil, then lower heat and cook slowly for 2 hours or until tender, and water is reduced to about a cup. Young, tender greens cook in less time than older plants. Greens should not be greasy but tasty and seasoned. More salt may be added if necessary. If too much water is used much of the food value is lost.

SWEET POTATO CASSEROLE

2 cups cooked mashed
  sweet potatoes
2 eggs
1 cup milk

1/2 teaspoon nutmeg
1 cup sugar
1/2 teaspoon cinnamon
1 Stick margarine

Mix sweet potatoes, eggs, milk, nutmeg, sugar, cinnamon, and butter together in mixer until smooth. Pour into baking dish. May be topped with chopped pecans. Bake at 400 degrees for 20 minutes.

COMPANY SWEET POTATOES

3 cups mashed sweet potatoes
1 cup sugar
1/2 cup milk

1/3 cup butter
2 eggs
1 teaspoon of vanilla

TOPPING
1 cup coconut
1 cup chopped nuts
1 cup brown sugar

1/3 cup flour
1/3 cup butter, melted

Mix sweet potatoes, sugar, milk, butter, eggs, and vanilla. Pour into baking dish. Mix coconut, nuts, brown sugar, and flour. Add melted butter. Sprinkle over potatoes. Bake at 375 degrees until brown; about 25 minutes.

POTATO CAKES

6 medium potatoes, pared
  (2 pounds)
1 small onion, grated
4 strips crisp bacon
  crumbled
2 tablespoons all-purpose
  flour

2 eggs, beaten
1 1/2 teaspoons salt
Dash of pepper
Dash of nutmeg
2 tablespoons chopped parsley
Butter or margarine

Peel potatoes and cover with cold water. Drain. Grate at once and drain. Mix potatoes, onion, flour, bacon, eggs, and seasonings, blending well. Heat butter (enough to be 1/4 inch deep) in skillet. Just before butter turns brown, drop in 1/3 cup batter for each pancake and flatten. When golden brown on one side, turn and brown on other side. Place on paper towel to drain. Keep warm while frying remaining pancakes.

Yield: 6 servings

RICH POTATOES

6 large potatoes (Idaho)
2 teaspoons salt
1 cup butter, divided
1 cup heavy cream

1 teaspoon coarse black
  pepper
1 cup shredded Gruyere
  or Cheddar cheese

Bake potatoes until soft. Split lengthwise and scoop the pulp into a mixing bowl, scraping the shells well. Leave the potatoes just as they were scooped from the shell; do not mash or chop. Soften 3/4 cup of the butter and add along with salt, pepper and cream. Mix lightly and transfer to a flat baking dish. Dot with remaining 4 tablespoons of butter and sprinkle with cheese. Bake at 375 degrees for 15 minutes.
Chopped bell pepper, onions or crumbled bacon may be added.

Yield: 6 servings

122

HASH BROWN POTAOTES

1 large onion, finely chopped
1/4 cup margarine
2 bay leaves
3/4 teaspoon paprika

3 large potatoes, peeled
  cooked, sliced
1/8 teaspoon garlic powder
Salt to taste

Preheat oven to 475. Combine onion, margarine and bay leaves in an 8x8-inch baking dish. Cover and bake 10 to 12 minutes or until onions are transparent. Add remaining ingredients, mixing lightly to combine. Bake uncovered for 15 minutes or until golden brown, stirring occasionally. Use bay leaves as garnish.

Yield: 6 servings.

TOMATOES AND OKRA

1-1/2 cups fresh okra, cut in
  1/2-inch slices
2 tablespoons salad oil
1 teaspoon all-purpose flour
1/4 teaspoon pepper
1/2 cup chopped onion

1/2 cup chopped green pepper
1 tablespoon sugar
3/4 teaspoon salt
3 tomatoes, peeled and
  quartered

Cook okra in a small amount of salted water for 10 minutes. Cover while cooking. Drain. Cook onion and pepper in oil until tender. Do not brown. Blend in flour, sugar, salt and pepper. Add tomatoes and okra. Cook over low heat until vegetables are hot. Stir as little as possible.

SCALLOPED POTATOES

5 cups cooked, sliced
  potatoes
2 cups cottage cheese
1 cup sour cream

1/4 cup chopped onions
2 teaspoons salt
1/2 cup cheese, shredded

Mix cottage cheese, sour cream, onion and salt. Carefully fold into potaotes. Place in a 1 1/2 quart casserole and top with cheese. Bake 40 minutes at 350 degrees.

Yield: 8 servings

OUR FAMOUS MACARONI AND CHEESE

Maccaroni
2 cups milk
2 eggs, beaten

Salt and pepper to taste
1 to 1 1/4 pounds coarsley
  grated cheese

Cook and drain enough macaroni to fill a medium size casserole 1/3 full. Mix cheese, macaroni, eggs and milk. Be sure. to have enough cheese to cover the top well. Bake in a 300 degree oven about 30 minutes until cheese milk is well set. Then broil at 400 degrees until brown on top. (I use a good Wisconsin cheese or a mild New York cheese.

Cakes

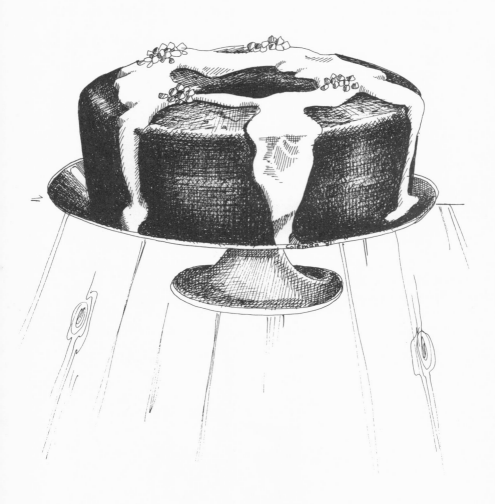

CAKES

FROSTINGS

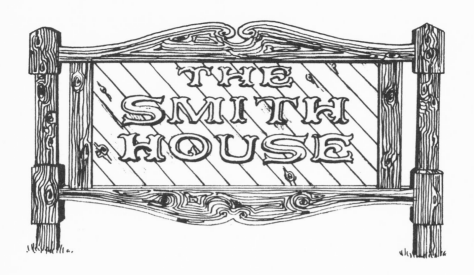

CAKES

QUEEN ELIZABETH CAKE

1/4 cup butter
1 cup sugar
2 eggs
1 1/2 cups flour
1 teaspoon vanilla

1/2 cup chopped nuts
1 cup boiling water
1 cup chopped dates
1 teaspoons baking soda

ICING
5 tablespoons sugar
5 tablespoons evaporated milk

2 tablespoons butter
Toasted coconut and nuts

Pour boiling water over chopped dates. Let stand until cool and then add baking soda. Cream butter and sugar well. Add eggs, flour, vanilla and nuts. Add date mixture. Pour into a long flat pan or a loaf pan and bake at 350 degrees for 25 to 30 minutes. Combine sugar, milk, and butter in pan and boil until thick, approximately 3 minutes, spread on top of cake and sprinkle with coconut and nuts.

APPLE CAKE (APPLE KUCHEN)

1/2 cup butter or
  margarine, softened
1 package of yellow cake mix
1/2 cup flaked coconut
1 (**20 ounce**) can pie-sliced
  apples, well drained

1/2 cup sugar
1 teaspoon cinnamon
1 cup dairy sour cream
2 egg yolks or 1 egg

Heat oven to 350. Cut butter into cake mix (dry) until crumbly. Mix in coconut. Pat mixture lightly in ungreased baking pan, 13x9x2 inches, buiding up edges slightly. Bake 10 minutes.

Arrange apple slices on warm crust. Sprinkle mixture of sugar and cinnamon on apples. Blend sour cream and egg yolks; drizzle over apples. (Topping will not completely cover apples). Bake 25 minutes or until edges are light brown. Do not over bake. Serve warm.

Yield: 12 servings.

APPLE STRUDEL

6 large or 8 medium apples
1/2 teaspoon cinnamon
1/2 cup margarine
1 cup chopped pecans

1 cup granulated sugar
1/2 cup brown sugar
1 cup flour

Peel and slice apples, place in buttered baking pan (9 x 13"). Mix cinnamon and granulated sugar. Sprinkle over apples. Cream brown sugar and margarine. Add flour and nuts and pour over thinly sliced apples. Bake at 350 degrees for 30 to 40 minutes.

APPLESAUCE CAKE I

3 1/2 cups plain flour
  divided
2 sticks margarine
2 cups sugar
1 teaspoon baking soda
1 cup applesauce
3 large eggs

1 teaspoon cloves
1 teaspoon allspice
1 teaspoon cinnamon
1/2 teaspoon salt
2 cups nuts chopped
  (not too fine)
1 pound box dark raisins

Dredge raisins and nuts in 1/2 cup of flour - set aside. Cream margarine and sugar. Combine soda and warm applesauce (not hot) and add to mixture. Add eggs one at a time. It is better if they are room temperature. Sift 3 cups of flour, cloves, salt, allspice and cinnamon and add to batter. Stir in nuts and raisins. Pour into greased and floured tube pan or two loaf pans. Bake at 300 degrees for 2 hours or until done. Leave in pan 15 minutes before turning out.

MARSHMALLOW FUDGE CAKE

1/2 cup butter, softened
1 cup sugar
4 eggs
1 teaspoon vanilla
1 cup self-rising flour

1 (16 ounce) can chocolate
  syrup
1 cup chopped nuts
1 (7 ounce) jar marshmallow
  cream

FUDGE-TOPPING
2 cups sugar
1/2 cup cocoa
1 tablespoon corn syrup

1/2 cup butter
1/2 cup milk

Cream butter and sugar until smooth. Add eggs one at a time, beating after each one. Add vanilla, flour and chocolate syrup, mixing well. Fold in nuts in 13x9 pan, bake at 350 degrees for 30 minutes. Spread marshmallow cream over hot cake. Then pour on fudge topping.

Combine sugar and cocoa. Add syrup, butter and milk and bring to a boil. Boil 1 minute. Remove from heat and beat 1 minute. Pour on cake.

APPLESAUCE-OATMEAL CAKE

1 1/4 cups canned sweetened
  applesauce
3/4 cups quick or old
  fashioned oats, uncooked
1 cup raisins
1/2 cup butter
3/4 cup brown sugar
  firmly packed

1 egg
1 1/2 cups sifted all purpose
  flour
1 teaspoon soda
3/4 teaspoon salt
1 teaspoon cinnamon
1/4 teaspoon cloves

VANILLA ICING
2 tablespoons butter or
  or margarine
Dash of salt
1/4 cup milk

2 1/4 cups sifted confectioners
  sugar
1/2 teaspoon vanilla

Heat together applesauce, oats, and raisins. Cover and set aside for 20 minutes. Whip butter until light and fluffy. Add sugar, egg and mix well. Sift together flour, soda, salt, cinnamon, and cloves. Stir dry ingredients into batter. Add applesauce mixture and mix thoroughly. Pour batter into greased and floured 9-inch square baking pan. Bake in oven 350 degrees for 50 to 55 minutes. Cool in pan on wire rack. Frost with vanilla icing.

ICING: Whip butter and salt until light and fluffy. Add milk. Gradually add confectioners sugar. Stir in vanilla.

BUTTERNUT CAKE

1 cup shortening
4 eggs
2 teaspoons baking powder
1 teaspoon butternut flavor

2 cups sugar
3 cups flour
1 cup milk

Cream shortening, sugar and eggs. Sift flour and baking powder together. Add half of milk and half of flour mixture. Beat well and add rest of milk, flour and flavoring. Pour in two 10-inch greased and floured pans. Bake 35 minutes at 350 degrees.

PEANUT BUTTER FUDGE CAKE

3/4 cup butter or margarine
1 cup peanut butter
  smooth or crunchy
2 1/4 cups sugar
1 1/2 teaspoons vanilla
3 eggs

3 (1 ounce) squares unsweetened
  chocolate, melted
3 cups sifted cake flour
1 1/2 teaspoons baking soda
3/4 teaspoon salt
1 1/2 cups ice water

Cream butter, peanut butter, sugar and vanilla. Add eggs and beat until fluffy. Add melted chocolate, blend well. Sift together flour, soda and salt. Add alternately with water to peanut butter-chocolate mixture. Pour into 3, 8 inch greased layer pans or a 10 inch greased tube pan. Bake in moderate oven, 350 degrees, until done, about 30 to 35 minutes for layer pans, 55 to 50 minutes for tube pan. Cool and frost with peanut butter frosting.

PEANUT BUTTER FUDGE FROSTING

2 (1 ounce) squares
  unsweetened chocolate
1/2 cup peanut butter

2 cups sugar
1 cup light cream

Combine ingredients in a heavy sauce pan. Boil over high heat 3 minutes without stirring. Reduce heat and cook until it reaches soft ball stage (238 degrees). Cool, beat until creamy and of spreading consistency. Add more cream if too thick. Spread sides of cake first, leaving top until last.

BROWN SUGAR POUND CAKE

1 box light brown sugar
1 cup white sugar
1 cup solid all-vegetable
  shortening
1 stick margarine or butter
5 large eggs

1 cup milk
1 cup self-rising flour
2 cups plain flour
1 teaspoon vanilla
1/2 teaspoon maple flavoring
1 cup chopped pecans

Cream sugars, shortening, and butter well. Add eggs one at a time beating well after each. Combine flours and add alternately with milk. Add flavoring and nuts. Pour into a large tube pan and bake at 250 degrees for 2 hours or 325 degrees for 1 1/2 hours. DO NOT OPEN OVEN DOOR BEFORE COOKING TIME IS UP.

PECAN POUND CAKE

2 cups shortening
3 cups sugar
10 eggs
3 cups flour, divided
1 teaspoon salt

1 teaspoon vanilla
1 teaspoon butternut flavoring
1 teaspoon almond
2 cups chopped nuts
1/4 cup evaporated milk

Mix shortening and sugar and let stand overnight. Next morning cream mixture and add eggs one at a time, beating after each addition. Add 2 3/4 cups flour, salt, flavorings and milk. Mix well. Dredge nuts in remaining 1/4 cup flour and fold in last. Bake in a large greased tube pan at 325 degrees for 1 hour and 20 minutes or until done.

POUND CAKE

2 cups sugar
1 cup solid all vegetable
   shortening
1/2 teaspoon salt

6 large eggs
2 cups flour
1 teaspoon vanilla
1 teaspoon almond

Cream sugar and shortening making sure it is well creamed. Add 3 eggs, one at a time mixing well. Combine flour and salt. Add one cup of flour and then add other 3 eggs, one at a time. Add other cup of flour and mix well. Add flavorings and pour batter into a greased (but not floured) tube pan. Bake for 1 hour at 325 degrees.
Be sure to cream sugar and shortening well and to mix well after each addition of eggs, flour and flavoring.

SOUR CREAM POUND CAKE

2 sticks margarine or butter
3 cups sugar
3 cups cake flour
1/4 teaspoon soda
6 eggs

1 cup sour cream
1 teaspoon vanilla extract
1 teaspoon lemon extract
1 cup coconut, optional

Cream margarine, add sour cream, then sugar - 1/2 cup at a time. Mix flour and soda. Add flour mixture, 1/2 cup at a time, alternately with eggs, finishing with egg. Beat well after each addition. Stir in flavoring and coconut. Bake in greased 10 inch tube pan at 300 degrees for 1 hour and 45 minutes to 2 hours.

ORANGE POUND CAKE

2 cups plain flour
1 cup vegetable shortening
1 3/4 cup sugar
5 eggs

1/3 cup orange juice
  (fresh or frozen)
1 teaspoon vanilla

Grease, flour and line bottom of tube pan. Cream sugar and shortening. Add eggs one at a time beating well. Sift flour three times and add alternating with liquid, beginning and ending with dry ingredients. Bake for one hour at 350 degrees. Use your favorite frosting.

GERMAN CHOCOLATE POUND CAKE

1 bar sweet German chocolate
2 cups sugar
1 cup shortening
4 eggs
2 teaspoons vanilla

2 teaspoons butter flavoring
1 cup buttermilk
3 cups sifted cake flour
1/2 teaspoon soda
1 teaspoon salt

Partially melt chocolate over hot water. Remove and stir fast until melted. Let cool. Cream sugar and shortening, add eggs, flavorings, and buttermilk. Sift together flour, soda and salt. Add to shortening and mix well. Blend in chocolate. Pour into a well greased and floured 9 inch tube pan. Bake at 300 degrees about 1 1/2 hours. Remove from pan while hot and place under tightly covered container until thoroughly cooled.

COCONUT POUND CAKE

3 cups cake flour, sifted
1/2 teaspoon salt
1 1/2 cups vegetable
   shortening
1 cup coconut

1 teaspoon baking powder
1 cup milk
2 1/2 cups sugar
5 eggs
1 tablespoon coconut flavoring

Sift flour, baking powder and salt together twice. Cream shortening and sugar for ten minutes. Add eggs, one at a time, beating after each addition. Add flour mixture alternately with milk, beating after each addition. Stir in coconut and flavoring. Place in cold oven and bake 1 hour and 25 minutes at 325 degrees.

SOUR CREAM COFFEE CAKE

3/4 cup butter or margarine,
   softened
1 1/2 cups sugar
3 eggs
1 teaspoon vanilla

3 cups plain flour
1 1/2 teaspoons baking powder
1 1/2 teaspoons soda
1/4 teaspoon salt
1 1/2 cups sour cream

TOPPING AND FILLING
1/2 cup brown sugar, packed
1/2 cup finely chopped nuts

1 1/2 teaspoon cinnamon

In large mixing bowl combine butter, sugar, eggs, and vanilla. Beat on medium speed for 2 minutes. Combine flour, baking powder, soda and salt. Add to butter mixture alternately with sour cream. In separate bowl combine filling ingredients. Spread 1/3 of batter, about 2 cups, in a greased tube pan. Sprinkle with 1/3 of filling mixture, about 6 tablespoons. Repeat layers twice. Bake in a 350 degree oven for 60 minutes or until wooden pick inserted in center comes out clean. Cool slightly in pan before removing.

Yield: 15 servings

WHOLE WHEAT CARROT CAKE

2 eggs
1/2 cup warmed honey or
  maple syrup
3/4 cup oil
1/4 cup buttermilk
1 1/2 cups grated carrots

1/2 cup chopped nuts
1 1/4 cups whole wheat
  pastry flour
1 teaspoon salt
1 teaspoon soda
1 tablespoon cinnamon

Preheat oven to 300 degrees and grease an 8x8 inch pan. In a mixing bowl, beat eggs and add honey, oil and buttermilk until well blended. Stir in carrots and nuts. In a separate bowl, sift together flour, salt, soda, and cinnamon. Fold into carrot mixture and mix well. Do not beat. Pour batter into pan and bake at 300 degrees for 1 hour. Remove from oven and allow to cool for 10 minute

STRAWBERRY PRESERVE CAKE

1 box yellow cake mix

1 large carton of whipped,
  frozen topping

FILLING
1 small package coconut
  macaroon cookies
1 small jar of strawberry preserves

2 packages of frozen
  strawberries

Crush macaroon cookeis (1 1/2 cups) and mix in strawberries and preserves and set aside for filling.

Prepare cake in the usual manner using round cake pans. After cake has cooled split each layer in half to make 4 layers. Spread the filling between 3 layers and on top of the cake. Ice with whipped topping and decorate with strawberry halves.

Keep refrigerated and serve cold.

RED VELVET CAKE

1 cup shortening
2 eggs
2 tablespoons cocoa
1 teaspoon vanilla
1 teaspoon salt
1 tablespoon vinegar

1 1/2 cups sugar
2 1/2 cups plain flour,
  sifted 3 times
1 cup buttermilk
1/4 cup red food coloring
1 teaspoon soda

ICING:
1 cup milk
7 teaspoons flour
1 cup butter

1 cup confectioners sugar
1 teaspoon vanilla

CAKE:
Cream sugar and shortening until fluffy, add eggs and beat 1 minute. Put vanilla in buttermilk and add alternately with flour to above ingredients. Make paste of coloring, cocoa and salt and add to mixture. Mix vinegar and soda in cup and add. Bake in two 8-inch pans for 30 minutes at 350 degrees. Cool 15 minutes and split each layer with a thread and ice in 4 layers.

ICING:
Cook the milk and flour together until thick. Refrigerate until later. Cream together the butter and powdered sugar. Add vanilla. Blend slowly into flour-milk mixture. Ice cake sparingly.

DATE AND BLACK WALNUT CAKE

1 pound dates, pitted
2 teaspoons baking soda
2 cups boiling water
2 cups sugar
4 tablespoons butter
  or margarine

2 eggs
3 1/2 cups flour
2 teaspoons vanilla
1 cup black walnuts,
  finely chopped

ICING:
1 cup brown sugar
1 cup white sugar
1 cup half and half cream

Dash of salt
1 tablespoon butter
  or margarine

Chop dates into a bowl and sprinkle with baking soda. Pour boiling water over dates and let stand. In another bowl beat eggs, sugar and butter. To this add flour and date mixtures alternately. Stir in vanilla and black walnuts. Bake in 3 layers at 350 degrees, 35 to 40 minutes.
ICING:
Place brown sugar, white sugar, cream and salt in saucepan, and cook to soft ball stage. Add butter and beat until light. Spread on cooled cake.

SWEET POTATO CAKE

1 1/2 cups cooking oil
2 cups sugar
4 eggs, separated
4 tablespoons hot water
2 1/2 cups plain flour
3 teaspoons baking powder
1/4 teaspoon salt

1 teaspoon cinnamon
1 teaspoon nutmeg
1 1/2 cups raw sweet
   potatoes, grated
1 cup nuts,
   chopped fine
1 teaspoon vanilla

Blend sugar and oil. Add egg yolks and beat well. Add vanilla. Sift together flour, baking powder, salt, cinnamon and nutmeg. Add to sugar and egg mixture. Blend in potatoes and nuts. Fold in stiffly beaten egg whites. Pour into 3 well-greased and floured 9-inch cake pans. Bake at 350 degrees 25 to 30 minutes.

FRUIT COCKTAIL CAKE

2 eggs
1 1/2 cups sugar
2 cups plain flour
1 teaspoon soda

1/4 teaspoon salt
1 (no. 2) can fruit cocktail
1 teaspoon vanilla

Add sugar to beaten eggs and beat about 5 minutes more. Sift togther flour, soda and salt. Add dry ingredients, fruit cocktail and vanilla to eggs and sugar mixture. Blend well. Grease and flour oblong baking pan. Bake at 350 degrees for 30 minutes.
   Frost with a butter frosting and cover with coconut.

BUTTER FROSTING

Small can evaporated milk
3/4 cup sugar

1 stick margarine
1 small can Angel Flake Coconut

Boil milk, sugar, and margarine for 1 1/2 minutes. Add coconut. Spread on cake while hot.

ROTTEN CAKE

1 box yellow cake mix
FROSTING
1 pint sour cream
1 cup sugar
1 teaspoon vanilla

1 carton frozen whipped
  topping mix
2 large packages frozen
  coconut

Bake cake as directed on box for a two layer cake. Cool and slice each layer in half to make 4 thin layers. Combine sugar, sour cream, vanilla and coconut. (Reserve 1 cup of sour cream for side frosting.) Spread between layers. Combine 1 cup sour cream and whipped topping mix Spread on top and sides of cake. Sprinkle with coconut. Refrigerate in tightly covered container for 3 days.

BUTTER PECAN-BANANA PUDDING CAKE

1/2 cup mashed bananas
1 package yellow cake mix,
  2 layer size
1 package butter pecan
  flavored instant pudding
  and pie filling, 4 serving size

4 eggs
1 cup water
1/4 cup oil
1/2 cup finely chopped nut,
  optional

GLAZE
1 tablespoon hot milk
  or water

1 cup sifted powdered sugar

Blend all ingredients in large mixing bowl. Beat 4 minutes at medium speed. Pour into greased and floured 10 inch bundt pan. Bake at 350 degrees for 50 minutes or until cake springs back when lightly pressed and pulls away from sides. Do not underbake. Cool in pan 15 minutes, remove and cool on rack. Top with confectioners sugar glaze and additional bananas, sliced.

GLAZE: Stir hot milk into powdered sugar and drizzle over cake.

HOLIDAY JAM CAKE

2 cups sugar
1 cup shortening
3 eggs
1 cup buttermilk
1 cup berry jam
3 cups flour
1 teaspoon soda

1 cup chopped nuts
1 cup raisins
1 cup ground coconut
1 large apple, grated
Chopped dates, if desired
1 1/2 teaspoon salt

TOPPING:
2 cups sugar
2 tablespoons flour
1 cup nuts, chopped
1 cup raisins
Cherries

1 1/2 cups milk
1 stick butter
1 cup grated coconut
1 apple, grated

Cream sugar and shortening, add eggs. Combine jam and buttermilk, add alternately with sifted flour, soda and salt. Fold in nuts and fruits last. Mix well. Bake in 3 layer cake pans 30-40 minutes at 350 degrees.

ICING

Mix sugar, flour, milk and butter in saucepan. Cook over medium heat until thick. Stir constantly. Remove from heat and add nuts, raisins, coconut and apple. Spread between each layer and on top. Decorate top with cherries.

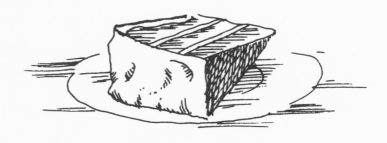

SKILLET UPSIDE DOWN CAKE

1/4 cup butter
3/4 cup brown sugar

1 cup pecans
8 canned pineapple slices

Melt butter in 9 inch skillet. Remove from heat. Sprinkle brown sugar and nuts over bottom. Arrange fruit on sugar. Prepare cake.

CAKE

2 eggs
1/4 teaspoons salt
1 cup sugar
1/2 cup rich milk

1 tablespoon melted shortening
1 teaspoon vanilla
1 cup sifted cake flour
1 tablespoon baking powder

Beat eggs until light. Continue beating and gradually add salt and sugar. Heat milk to boiling point and add butter. Beat into egg mixture and add vanilla. Resift flour with baking powder and add, beating quickly until blended. Pour batter over fruit. Bake in 325 degree oven for about 30 minutes. Turn out while warm. Serve upside down.

TUNNEL OF FUDGE CAKE

1 1/2 cup butter or margarine
6 eggs
1 1/2 cup sugar
2 cups flour

1 package double fudge
    butter-cream frosting mix
2 cups chopped walnuts

Cream butter at high speed. Add eggs one at a time, beating well after each. Gradually add sugar. Stir in flour, frosting mix and walnuts. Pour into greased tube pan. Bake at 350 for 60 to 65 minutes. Cool for 2 hours.

SUPREME CREAM CAKE

1 cup shortening
5 eggs
1 teaspoon soda
1 (8 ounce) package cream
   cheese, softened
1 teaspoon vanilla

2 cups sugar
2 cups plain flour
1 1/2 cups buttermilk
1 cup coconut
1 cup chopped nuts

Cream sugar and shortening using electric mixer. Add eggs, one at a time beating well after each addition. Sift together flour and salt and add this to the batter alternately with milk. Stir in cream cheese and vanilla. Beat 1 minute. Fold in coconut and nuts. Divide evenly into 3 greased and floured layer cake pans. Bake at 350 degrees for 35 to 40 minutes. Frost with coconut-pecan frosting.

COCONUT PECAN FROSTING

1/2 pound butter
2 cups sugar
6 egg yolks, well beaten
1/2 cup sweet milk

2 cups chopped pecans
2 cups raisins
2 cups coconut
1 teaspoon vanilla

Mix butter, sugar, egg yolks and milk. Cook over low heat, stirring occasionally until it looks syrupy and glossy. Then add nuts, raisins, coconut and vanilla. Spread between layers and on top. Ice sides of cake with white frosting.

WHITE BUTTER FROSTING

6 tablespoons margarine
1/8 teaspoon salt
1 pound powdered sugar, sifted

2 teaspoons vanilla
5 tablespoons milk

Melt margarine. Pour all ingredients into bowl. Stir to blend. Then beat at high speed for one minute.

CHOCOLATE FROSTING

1/4 cup shortening
1/4 teaspoon salt
2/3 cup milk
1/2 teaspoon chocolate flavor

1/2 cup cocoa
1 box powdered sugar, sifted
1 teaspoon vanilla

In a saucepan melt shortening, add cocoa, salt and milk. Put sifted sugar in bowl. Then pour cocoa mixture into sugar. Beat until creamy. Add flavorings.

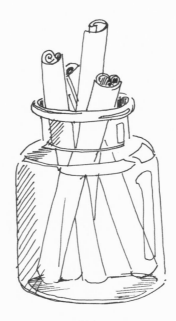

COOKIES

COOKIES

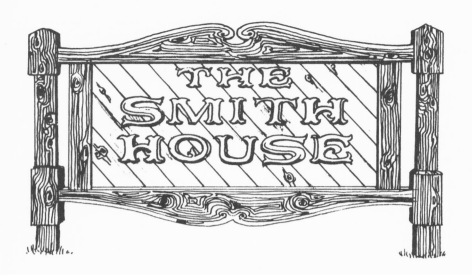

COOKIES

SMITH HOUSE FAMOUS BANANA FRITTERS

2 1/3 cups all-purpose flour
1/2 cup sugar
1/2 teaspoon soda
1/2 teaspoon salt
1/2 teaspoon baking powder

2 eggs
2 (13 ounce) cans of evaporated
  milk
12 bananas

Sift flour, baking powder, soda and salt together. Beat eggs and sugar together. Add milk alternately with sifted dry ingredients to egg mixture. Beat after each addition.

This mixture should be a thin batter. Peel bananas and quarter. Dip bananas in batter and drop into hot oil. Fry until golden brown. This batter can be used for apple fritters by adding spices, 1/2 teaspoon cinnamon, 1/2 teaspoon nutmeg, and the sliced or chopped apples.

PUMPKIN FRITTERS

5 eggs	3 cups bread flour
1 1/2 cups sugar	1 (no. 2 1/2) can pumpkin
1/2 teaspoon salt	8 teaspoons vanilla
1/4 nutmeg	2 teaspoons baking powder
1 1/4 teaspoon cinnamon	Melted butter

Beat eggs and mix with sugar, salt, spices and flour. Beat until mixture becomes smooth and fluffy. Add pumpkin, vanilla, and baking powder. Whip until thoroughly mixed. Fry in skillet in melted butter until fritter becomes brown on both sides. Fry slowly; otherwise, fritter will not be done in middle.   Yield: about 4 dozen.

MELT-AWAYS

1 stick butter or margarine	1 package butterscotch morsels
1 1/2 cups graham cracker crumbs	1 can flake coconut
1 package chocolate morsels	1 cup chopped nuts
	1 can condensed milk

Melt butter in bottom of 13x9x2 inch pan. Sprinkle crumbs over butter in pan. Add layers of chocolate morsels, butterscotch, nuts, and coconut. Pour condensed milk over top and bake at 350 degrees for 25 minutes. Cool in pan 10 to 15 minutes then cut into bars.

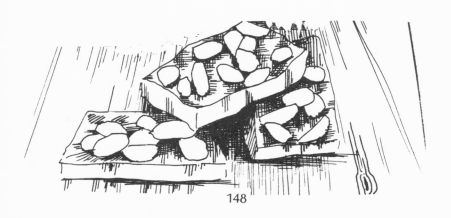

CHOCOLATE COCONUT CANDIES

3/4 cup mashed potatoes
1 (16 ounce) box powdered
   sugar
4 cups flaked coconut
1 teaspoon almond extract

Chocolate coating
2 tablespoons soft margarine
2 tablespoons cornsyrup
3 tablespoons water
1 package chocolate fudge
   frosting mix

Mix potatoes, sugar, coconut and almond well. Drop mixture by heaping teaspoonsful onto wax paper and roll into balls. Chill 1/2 to 1 hour or until firm. If mixture is too soft to form ball, chill before shaping. In top of double boiler, mix margarine, corn syrup and water. Stir in dry frosting and mix until smooth. Heat over rapidly boiling water for 5 minutes, stirring occasionally. Using tongs or forks, dip balls into chocolate coating. Turn to coat evenly. (Keep coating over hot water while dipping balls.) Remove balls from coating and place on waxed paper or wire rack. Chill until firm.

Yield: 5 dozen

CRISP ALMOND FINGERS

2 egg whites
1/3 cup sugar
1/4 teaspoon almond extract
1/4 teaspoon salt

1/2 cup soft butter or margarine
1 teaspoon vanilla
1 1/2 cup sifted all-purpose flour
2/3 cup diced (unblanched)
   almonds

Lightly beat egg whites. Set aside 1 tablespoon for tops of cookies. Cream butter and sugar well. Add egg whites, vanilla and almond extract. (Batter will look curdled.) Blend in flour and salt. Set aside 2 tablespoons almond for tops of cookies; mix remainder into dough. Shape into a small rectangle on waxed paper, wrap in the paper, and chill thoroughly 1 to 2 hours. Roll dough out between sheets of waxed paper to a 7½-inch square, 1/2 inch thick. With a floured knife, cut in thirds from one side, and into 8 slices from the other. Making 24 fingers. Place on lightly greased baking sheet. Brush tops with the reserved egg white, and sprinkle with almonds. Bake above oven center at 350 degrees 20 to 25 minutes, until very lightly browned. Cool on wire racks.

Yield: 24 cookies

PEANUT BUTTER
CHOCOLATE CHIP BROWNIES

3/4 cup peanut butter
1 1/2 cup sugar
4 eggs
3 cups sifted all-purpose
  flour
1 teaspoon salt
1/2 cup margarine

1 1/2 cup firmly packed light
  brown sugar
2 teaspoons vanilla
1 tablespoon baking powder
1 (6 ounce) package chocolate
  chips

Cream peanut butter and butter until soft and creamy. Gradually blend in sugar and brown sugar. Beat in eggs one at a time. Add vanilla. Sift flour, baking powder and salt and add all at once. Beat until smooth and well blended. Stir in chocolate chips. Spread mixture into a greased and floured 13X9X2 inch pan. Bake in a preheated oven 350 degrees for 35 to 40 minutes. Cool in pan and then cut into squares.

PECAN LOG ROLL

1 (6 ounce) package
  butterscotch morsels
1/2 cup chopped pecans
Additional chopped pecans

1/3 cup condensed milk
1/2 teaspoon vanilla
1 egg white, slightly beaten

Melt morsels over hot (not boiling) water. Remove from heat. Stir in condensed milk, vanilla and pecans. Chill until firm enough to handle. Roll tightly on waxed paper to form 12-inch roll. Brush with egg whites, roll in additional chopped pecans. Chill and slice.

CARROT COOKIES

1 cup shortening (part soft
  butter)
3/4 cup sugar
2 eggs
1 cup mashed cooked carrots

2 cups flour
2 teaspoons baking powder
1/2 teaspoon salt
3/4 cup shredded coconut
Orange Butter Icing

ORANGE BUTTER ICING
3 tablespoons soft butter
1 1/2 cups confectioners sugar

2 teaspoons grated orange peel
About 1 tablespoon orange juice

Heat oven to 400. Mix shortening, sugar, eggs and carrots. Blend in flour, baking powder and salt. Stir in coconut. Drop dough by teaspoonfuls about 2 inches apart onto lightly greased baking sheet.
Bake 8 to 10 minutes or until no imprint remains when touched lightly. Immediately remove from baking sheet. Cool. Frost with Orange Butter Icing.

Blend butter and sugar. Stir in orange peel and juice. Beat until frosting is smooth and of spreading consistency. Frost cookies. Yield: 4 dozen.

SOFT MOLASSES COOKIES

1 cup shortening
1 1/2 cups molasses
1/4 cup sugar
4 cup sifted flour
1 1/2 teaspoons salt

2 teaspoons soda
2 teaspoons cinnamon
1 1/2 teaspoons ginger
1/2 teaspoon cloves
1 egg

Melt shortening in a saucepan large enough for mixing dough. Stir in molasses and sugar; cool. Sift together flour, salt, soda, cinnamon, ginger and cloves. Mix a small amount of flour into shortening mixture. Beat in egg. Add remaining flour and blend until smooth. Chill dough about 2 hours. Shape into 1 1/4 inch balls. Place on baking sheets about 2 inches apart. Bake in a moderate oven 350 degrees about 15 minutes. Remove to wire racks. While still warm, spread half the cookies with a confectioners' sugar icing.

Yield: 4 dozen

COCONUT POMPONS

1 cup margarine
1/2 cup sugar
2 teaspoons vanilla
2 cups sifted flour

1/4 teaspoon salt
1/2 pound pecan halves
Chopped, shredded coconut

Cream together margarine, sugar and vanilla until light and fluffy. Sift together flour and salt. Add to creamed mixture and blend thoroughly. Shape dough around pecan halves to form one inch balls. Roll in shredded coconut. Place on an ungreased baking sheet. Bake in a slow oven 325 about 20 minutes. Remove to wire rack and cool.

Yield: 6 dozen

TOFFEE

1 cup chopped pecans
3/4 cup brown sugar, packed
1/2 cup butter or margarine

1/2 cup semi-sweet chocolate
   pieces

Butter a 9x9x2 inch baking pan. Spread pecans in bottom of pan. Heat sugar and butter to boiling, stirring constantly. Boil over medium heat for 7 minutes stirring the entire time. Immediately spread mixture evenly over nuts in pan. Sprinkle chocolate pieces over hot mixture; place flat baking sheet over pan containing mixture, so contained heat will melt chocolate. Using knife or spatula spread melted chocolate evenly over candy while hot, cut into 1 1/2 inch squares. Chill until firm.

Yield: 3 dozen.

APPLESAUCE COOKIES

1 3/4 cups quick oats
  uncooked
1 1/2 cups unsifted flour
1 teaspoon salt
1 teaspoon baking powder
1 teaspoon cinnamon
1/2 teaspoon nutmeg
1/2 teaspoon baking soda
1/2 cup butter, softened

1 cup brown sugar,
  firmly packed
1/2 cup granulated sugar
1 egg
3/4 cup applesauce
6 ounce package semi-sweet
  chocolate morsels
1 cup raisins
1 cup chopped nuts

Heat oven to 375. In small bowl, combine oats, flour, salt, baking powder, cinnamon, nutmeg and baking soda; set aside. In large bowl, cream butter, brown sugar and granulated sugar. Beat in egg. Gradually blend in flour mixture alternately with applesauce. Stir in semi-sweet chocolate morsels, raisins and nuts. Drop by level measuring tablespoonfuls onto greased cookie sheets. Bake at 375 for 14 minutes.

Yield: 5 dozen.

HONEY COOKIES

1/2 cup shortening
1/2 cup sugar
1/2 cup honey
1 egg
1/2 cup chopped nuts

2 1/2 cups sifted flour
1 teaspoon baking powder
1/4 teaspoon soda
1/4 teaspoon salt

Cream together shortening, sugar and honey until light and fluffy. Stir in egg. Add nuts and mix well. Sift together flour, baking powder, soda and salt. Add to honey mixture and blend well. Divide dough in half. Shape each half into a long roll. Wrap in waxed paper and chill in refrigerator about 2 hours. Cut into slices about 1/8 inch thick. Place slices on ungreased baking sheet. Bake in a hot oven 400 degrees 8 to 10 minutes.

Yield: 4 dozen cookies

POTATO DOUGHNUTS

Potato Buds instant puffs
  (enough for 2 servings)
3 eggs
3/4 cups sugar
3 tablespoons shortening
2 teaspoons vanilla

2 3/4 cups flour
4 teaspoons baking powder
1 teaspoon salt
1/4 teaspoon nutmeg
1/4 teaspoon cinnamon

Prepare Potato Buds instant puffs as directed on package for 2 servings except - omit butter and salt. Add eggs, sugar, shortening and vanilla. Beat thoroughly. Stir in flour, baking powder, salt, nutmeg and cinnamon. Turn onto generously floured board; knead about 10 times. Roll dough 1/3 inch thick. Let rest 20 minutes.

In deep fat fryer, heat fat or oil (3 to 4 inches) deep to 375 to 380 degrees. Cut dough with floured doughnut cutter. Fry doughnuts until brown; drain.

Yield: 1 1/2 dozen.

WHOLE WHEAT DOUGHNUTS

1/2 cup milk, scalded
1/3 cup butter
1/2 cup warmed honey
1/2 teaspoon salt
2 tablespoons warm potato
  water

1 teaspoon dry yeast
1/2 cup mashed potatoes
1 egg, well-beaten'
2 1/2 cups whole wheat flour
Softened butter and coconut
  for dusting

Combine milk, butter, honey, and salt. Stir well and cook to lukewarm. Dissolve yeast in potato water and add to milk mixture. Add potatoes and egg, then work in flour. Place in greased bowl, cover, and let rise about 1 hour, until light. Place on floured board and knead for 5 to 8 minutes. Roll to 1/2 inch thickness and cut into circles, using 3-inch doughnut cutter. Place on buttered cookie sheets, and let rise again for about 45 minutes. Preheat oven to 425. Bake doughnuts about 12 minute, until lightly browned. Remove from oven and brush immediately with butter and dust with coconut.   Yield: 1 1/2 dozen.

DREAM SQUARES

1/2 cup butter
1 1/2 cups brown sugar, divided
1 1/4 cups sifted all-purpose
   flour, divided
2 eggs
1 teaspoon vanilla

1/4 teaspoon salt
1/2 teaspoon baking powder
1 (4 ounce) can flaked coconut
2 1/2 cups sliced apples
1 cup chopped nut meats

Cream together butter, 1/2 cup brown sugar and 1 cup flour until crumbly. Pat out into greased 9x9x2" baking pan. Bake in moderate oven 350 degrees 20 minutes. Beat eggs, and vanilla and remaining 1 cup brown sugar, 1/4 cup flour, salt and baking powder. Mix well. Add apples, coconut and nut meats. Pour over baked crust. Return to oven bake 20 to 25 minutes.

Yield: 16 squares

155

SEMI-SWEET SOUR CREAM WAFERS

1/3 cup butter
1/3 cup shortening
2 cups brown sugar,
  firmly packed
1 tablespoon vanilla
1 egg
1/2 cup sour cream

3 1/2 cups sifted flour
1 teaspoon baking soda
1/2 teaspoon salt
1/2 teaspoon nutmeg
1 cup semi-sweet
  chocolate morsels, finely chopped

Cream together butter, shortening and sugar until light and fluffy. Add vanilla and egg. Beat well. Stir in sour cream. Sift together flour, soda, salt and nutmeg. Add to creamed mixture and blend well. Stir in chocolate. Line a 10 by 5 by 3 loaf pan with waxed paper. Pack dough firmly into pan. Chill overnight. Slice loaf lengthwise into thirds; then cut each third into slices 1/8 inch thick. Place on ungreased baking sheet. Bake in a hot oven 400 degrees 8 minutes.

Yield: 4 dozen

CRISP PEANUT BUTTER COOKIES

1 cup margarine
1 cup peanut butter
  creamy or crunchy
1 cup sugar
1 cup firmly packed brown
  sugar

2 eggs, beaten
1 teaspoon vanilla
2 1/2 cups sifted flour
1 teaspoon baking powder
1 teaspoon baking soda
1 teaspoon salt

Cream margarine, peanut butter and sugars. Mix in eggs and vanilla. Sift flour, baking powder, baking soda and salt together over creamed mixture. Stir until well blended. Chill dough until it can be easily handled. Shape into one inch balls. Place about two inches apart on greased cookie sheet. Flatten with floured bottom of glass or with floured fork, making crosswide pattern on each if fork is used. Bake in moderate oven 350 degrees until lightly browned, 12 to 15 minutes.

Yield: 6 dozen

Desserts

DESSERTS

DESSERTS

MOCHA MARVEL

1 1/2 cups (17) cream-filled
   chocolate sandwich cookies
   crushed
3 tablespoons butter or
   margarine, melted
1 (4 ounce) package vanilla
   soft-style whipped
   dessert mix
1 1/3 cups milk
1 teaspoon vanilla

1 (4 1/2 ounce) carton frozen
   whipped dessert topping
   thawed
1 teaspoon instant coffee
   (dissolved in 1 teaspoon
   water)
1 tablespoon brown sugar
1 (1 ounce) square
   unsweetened chocolate
   melted and cooled

Combine 1 1/4 cups crushed cookies (reserve 1/4 cup) and butter. Press crumbs into 10x6x2-inch baking dish. Prepare dessert mix using the 1 1/3 cups milk and vanilla. Fold in frozen whipped topping. Add dissolved coffee to brown sugar. Blend into half of whipped mixture. Spoon over crumb crust. Stir chocolate into remaining whipped mixture and spread over coffee layer. Top with reserved crumbs freeze.

Yield: 8 servings.

FROZEN MOCHA TOFFEE DESSERT

8 ladyfingers, split
2 tablespoons instant
  coffee crystals
1 tablespoon boiling water
1 quart vanilla ice cream
  softened

4 chocolate-covered toffee bars,
  frozen and crushed (1 cup)
1/2 cup whipping cream
2 tablespoons white creme
  de cacao

Line the bottom and 2 inches up sides of an 8-inch springform pan with the split ladyfingers, cutting to fit. Dissolve the coffee crystals in the 1 tablespoon boiling water. Cool. Stir together coffee, ice cream, and crushed candy. Spoon into springform pan; cover and freeze till firm. Before serving combine cream and creme de cacao; whip to soft peaks. Spread over top of frozen ice cream layer. Garnish with pieces of additional broken toffee bars, if desired.

Yield: 8 to 10 servings

OLD FASHIONED CHOCOLATE PUDDING

1 cup sugar
1/4 teaspoon salt
2 cups milk
1 teaspoon butter

1/3 cup flour
2 egg yolks
1/3 cup cocoa
1/2 teaspoon vanilla

Sift together sugar, salt, and flour. Put in top of a double boiler and stir in 1/3 cup milk and beaten egg yolks. Mix until well blended. Add remaining milk and cocoa and cook until thick, stirring constantly. Add butter and vanilla. To use for a pie, pour into a baked pie shell. Top with meringue and brown lightly. Cool before serving.

OLD FASHION BAKED CUSTARD

2 cups milk
3 eggs
1/2 teaspoon vanilla

1/2 cup sugar
Pinch of salt

Beat eggs, add sugar and mix well. Add milk, vanilla and salt. Beat lightly. Pour into individual cups. Preheat oven to 350 degrees. Place custard cup in pan of hot water and bake in oven for 30 minutes. Test with knife to make sure they are done in center.

CHERRY PUDDING

1 cup plain flour
1 cup sugar
1 teaspoon soda
1/2 teaspoon salt
1 egg

1 cup canned red tart
  cherries, plus enough liquid
  to fill cup
1/2 cup coarsley chopped nuts
1 tablespoon butter or margarine

Grease 9x9x2 inch baking pan. Mix all ingredients. Pour into pan. Bake about 40 minutes. Serve warm with topping if you wish.

RICE TUTTI FRUTTI

1 cup uncooked rice
2 1/2 cup water
1/2 teaspoon salt
1 cup sugar
1/2 teaspoon cinnamon

1 teaspoon vanilla
2 large oranges, cut crosswise
2 large bananas, cut up
2/3 cup chopped nuts
1 large apple, cut up

Cook rice in salted water. Mix sugar, cinnamon and vanilla with hot rice, cool. Add oranges, bananas, nuts, and apples. Chill. Serve.
Note: Pineapples, raisins or shredded coconut may be added as an extra.
This recipe comes from Ursula Karel, Orlando, Florida. She and her husband, Frank, have been making the Smith House Inn their vacation spot for the last 17 years.

BANANA COCONUT BETTY

2 cups fresh whole grain
   bread crumbs
1/3 cup melted butter
2 tablespoons honey
1/2 teaspoon cinnamon
1/2 cup grated, unsweetened
   coconut

4 medium-size bananas
   thinly sliced
1/2 teaspoon nutmeg
1 tablespoon grated lemon
   rind
1 cup light cream
2 tablespoons lemon juice

Preheat oven to 375, and grease a 1 1/2-quart casserole. Mix bread crumbs with butter. Arrange a third of the crumbs in the bottom of the prepared casserole. Cover with half of the bananas. Mix honey, nutmeg, cinnamon, and lemon peel. Drizzle half the mixture over the bananas. Layer another third of the crumbs, then the remaining bananas, and the rest of the honey mixture. Pour lemon juice over the whole mixture. Combine the remaining crumbs with coconut and sprinkle over the top of the casserole. Bake, uncovered, for about 35 minutes or until golden brown. Serve warm with light cream.

SWEET POTATO PUDDING

1/3 cup butter	1/2 cup chopped nuts
4 cups grated, raw,	1 cup raisins
sweet potatoes	1/2 teaspoon cloves
1/4 teaspoon salt	1 teaspoon allspice
2/3 cup honey	1 teaspoon cinnamon
1 1/2 cups milk	3 eggs, well beaten

In a medium-size saucepan, melt butter and add sweet potatoes, salt, honey, milk, nuts, raisins and spices. Place over low heat, and stir until mixture is well heated. Add eggs slowly, stirring constantly. Pour mixture into greased 2-quart casserole and bake in preheated 350 degree oven for 30 to 40 minutes. Serve hot or cold, with light cream, if desired.

STRAWBERRY YOGURT WHIP

1 (3 ounce) package	3/4 cup cold water
strawberry gelatin	1 (8 ounce) carton strawberry
1 cup boiling water	yogurt

Dissolve gelatin in boiling water. Add cold water and chill until slightly thickened. Add yogurt and beat with rotary beater until mixture is light and fluffy. Pour into punch cups or individual serving dishes. Chill about 2 hours.

Yield: 4 cups serving.

COCONUT-APPLE CRISP

4 medium-size apples, pared,
cored and thinly sliced
1/4 cup sugar
1/2 teaspoon ground cinnamon
1/2 cup chopped nuts
1/3 cup butter or margarine

1/3 cup sugar
1 egg
1 teaspoon vanilla
1/2 cup flaked coconut
1/2 cup sifted all-purpose
flour

Heat oven to 375. Place apple slices in shallow 1-quart dish. Sprinkle evenly with 1/4 cup sugar, cinnamon, and nuts. Cream butter and 1/3 cup sugar in small bowl. Add egg, vanilla, and coconut; mix thoroughly. Stir in flour gently. Spread batter evenly over apples. Bake 35 minutes or until crust is crisp and golden.

Yield: 6 to 8 servings.

PERFECT PEACH COBBLER

3 cups sliced fresh or
canned peaches
1 tablespoon lemon juice
1 cup sifted all-purpose
flour

1 cup sugar
1/2 teaspoon salt
1 egg, beaten
6 tablespoons butter or
margarine, melted

Arrange peaches on bottom of 10x6x1 1/2 inch baking dish. Sprinkle with lemon juice. Sift together flour, sugar, and salt. Add egg to dry ingredients, tossing with fork until crumbly. Sprinkle over peaches. Drizzle with butter. Bake 375 degrees for 35 to 40 minutes.

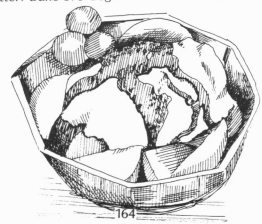

Pies

PIES

EGG CUSTARD PIE

4 eggs, separated
2 cups milk
1 teaspoon vanilla

1 cup sugar, divided
1/4 teaspoon salt
1 unbaked pastry shell

Combine beaten egg yolks with 3/4 cup sugar and beat until lemon colored. Slowly pour scalded milk into this egg mixture, stirring constantly. Add salt and vanilla. Dry the unbaked shell slightly before pouring in egg mixture. Bake 15 minutes at 400 degrees. Then reduce heat to 250 degrees and bake until custard is firm.
FOR MERINGUE: Beat egg whites with a dash of salt until stiff but not dry. Then beat in 1/4 cup sugar. Place on custard and bake to a golden brown at 300 degrees.

CHOCOLATE PIE

1 cup sugar
3 tablespoons cornstarch
1/4 teaspoon salt
1/2 cups chocolate morsels

2 cups milk
3 slightly beaten egg yolks
2 tablespoons butter
1 teaspoon vanilla

In saucepan combine sugar, cornstarch, and salt. Blend slightly beaten egg yolks and milk; stir into dry ingredients. Add melted chocolate and cook over medium heat; stirring constantly. Cook until mixture bubbles and thickens. Remove from heat, add butter and vanilla. Cook and pour into baked pie crust.

OLD FASHIONED BUTTERMILK PIE

1 (9 inch) pastry crust
3 eggs
2/3 cup buttermilk
2 cups sugar

1 tablespoon flour
1/2 cup butter, melted
1 teaspoon vanilla

Line a 9-inch pie plate with pastry. In mixing bowl, beat eggs until smooth. Add buttermilk and mix well. Add sugar, flour, butter and vanilla. Blend well. Pour into pastry-lined plate. Bake in preheated 375 degree oven for 1 hour, or until knife inserted in center comes out clean.

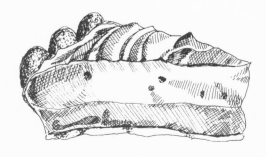

OLD-FASHIONED PUMPKIN PIE

Pie crust for nine inch pie
2 eggs
1 (16 ounce) can pumpkin
3/4 cup sugar
1/2 teaspoon salt

1 teaspoon cinnamon
1/2 teaspoon ginger
1/4 teaspoon cloves
1 (13 ounce) can evaporated
  milk

Heat oven to 425 degrees. Beat eggs slightly with rotary beater; beat in remaining ingredients. Pour into pastry-lined pie pan. Bake 15 minutes. Reduce oven temperature to 350 and bake 45 minutes longer or until knife inserted between center and edge comes out clean. Cool.

CHERRY BREEZE

1 cup cornflake crumbs
1/3 cup butter or margarine
  melted
1 (8 ounce) package cream
  cheese, softened
1 can condensed milk

1/2 cup reconstituted lemon
  juice (measure accurately)
1 teaspoon vanilla
1 (1 pound 5 ounces) cherry
  pie filling, chilled

Mix cornflake crumbs and butter thoroughly. Press firmly and evenly on bottom and sides of a 9 inch pie pan to form crust. Chill. Beat cream cheese until light and fluffy. Add condensed milk and blend thoroughly. Stir in lemon juice and vanilla. Turn into crust. Refrigerate 3-4 hours, or until firm. (Do not freeze). Top with chilled cherry pie filling before serving.   Yield: 8 servings

ALMOND CRUST CHERRY CREAM PIE

1 stick instant pie crust
  mix, or your own recipe
1/2 cup slivered almonds,
  finely chopped
1 (15 ounce) can condensed
  milk

1/3 cup lemon juice
1 teaspoon vanilla
1/2 teaspoon almond
1/2 cup whipping cream
  whipped

GLAZE
1 (16 ounce) can pitted sour
  cherries, drained
2/3 cup cherry juice

1/4 cup sugar
1 tablespoon cornstarch
2 to 3 drops red food coloring

Mix pastry mix as directed on package and add chopped almonds with the water. Prick sides of pie crust only. Bake as directed and cool. Combine condensed milk (must be condensed milk!), lemon juice, vanilla and almond. Stir until thoroughly mixed. Fold in whipped cream and spoon into cooled shell. Top with Cherry Glaze or use a prepared cherry pie filling.

Blend cherry juice with sugar and corn starch. Cook over low heat, stirring constantly, until mixture thickens and is clear. Add cherries and food coloring. Spread over cream filling. Chill 2 to 3 hours.

BANANA BREEZE

NO-BAKE CRUST
1/3 cup butter or margarine
1/4 cup sugar

1/2 teaspoon cinnamon
1 cup corn flake cereal crumbs

NO-COOK FILLING
1 (8 ounce) package cream
   cheese, softened
1 (15 ounce) can condensed
Milk (not evaporated)

1/3 cup bottled lemon juice
1 teaspoon vanilla
5 medium size ripe bananas
2 tablespoons lemon juice

In a small saucepan melt butter and add sugar and cinnamon. Stir constantly over low heat until bubbles form around edges of pan. Remove from heat, add cornflake crumbs and mix well. Press mixture evenly into a 9 inch pie pan to form crust. Chill.

Beat cream cheese until light and fluffy. Add condensed milk and blend thoroughly. Add 1/3 cup lemon juice and vanilla and stir until thickened. Slice 3 bananas and line crust. Pour filling into crust. Refrigerate 2 to 3 hours or until firm. (Do not freeze). Slice remaining bananas, dip in lemon juice and arrange on top of pie.

Yield: 8 servings

MILLION DOLLAR PIE

1 can condensed milk
1/4 cup lemon juice
1 box (2 envelopes) whipped
   topping mix
1 cup chopped nuts

1 small can crushed pineapple,
   drained
2 graham cracker crust
1 can coconut

Combine milk and juice set aside. Beat whipped topping mix following instructions on package. Add nuts and pineapple to condensed milk and juice. Pour into crust, top with coconut. Chill.

EXCELLENT PECAN PIE

3 eggs
3/4 cups sugar
3/4 cup white syrup

1 stick butter, melted
1 teaspoon vanilla
1 cup chopped pecans

Beat eggs thoroughly, add sugar and syrup. Mix melted butter into syrup mixture and add vanilla and nuts. Pour into unbaked pie shell. Bake 400 degrees for 10 minutes then at 300 for 30 minutes.

Yield: 1 pie

PECAN PIE

One (9 inch) pie crust
2 tablespoons butter, melted
3 eggs
1 cup sugar
1/2 teaspoon salt

1/2 cup dark corn syrup
1/2 cup whipping cream
1 teaspoon vanilla
1/4 cup brandy
1 cup pecan halves

In small mixer bowl, beat eggs, sugar, salt, butter, syrup and cream. Stir in vanilla, brandy and pecans. Pour into pastry-lined pie pan. Bake 40 to 50 minutes at 375 degrees or until filling is set and pastry is golden brown. Cool.

Yield: 8 to 10 servings

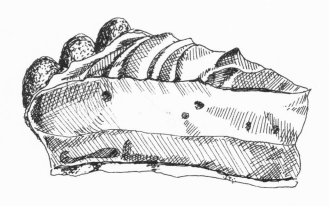

Beverages

BEVERAGES

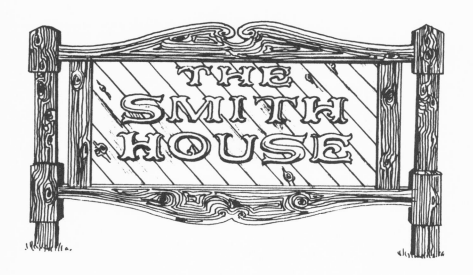

BEVERAGES

FRESH APPLE CIDER DRINK

2 quarts fresh apple cider
  or apple juice
1 to 1 1/2 quarts cranberry
  juice

1/2 cup brown sugar
1/2 teaspoon salt
4 cinnamon sticks
1 1/2 teaspoons whole cloves

Pour fruit juices into large coffee percolator. Place remaining ingredients in basket. Remove basket assembly upon completion of perking cycle. Makes 40 servings. This can be cooked on the stove on low setting. Wrap spices in cheese cloth, for easy removal. Juice should simmer for 30 minutes on low heat.

SUMMERTIME FRUIT PUNCH

3 cups fresh orange juice,
  strained
1 1/2 cups fresh lemon juice,
  strained
1 (48 ounce) bottle cranberry
  juice cocktail

Grated rind of 1 orange
Grated rind of 1 lemon
2 cups water
2 cups sugar
2 teaspoons almond extract
1 quart ginger ale

Combine orange and lemon rind, water, and sugar in a medium saucepan. Bring to a boil, and simmer 5 minutes. Let cool. Stir in almond extract and fruit juices. Pour over ice and stir in ginger ale.

Yield: 1 gallon.

MOCK PINK CHAMPAGNE

1/2 cup sugar
1 cup water
1 cup grapefruit juice
1/2 cup orange juice
1/4 cup grenadine syrup

1 (28 ounce) bottle ginger ale,
  chilled
Twists of lemon peel
Maraschino cherries with
  stems on

Combine sugar and water in saucepan. Simmer uncovered, stirring constantly, till sugar is dissolved, about 3 minutes, then cool. Mix with truit jucies and grenadine syrup in punch bowl. Chill. Just before serving, add ginger ale, pouring it slowly down side of bowl. Serve over ice in sherbet glasses. Trim each with peel and a cherry.   Yield: 6 cups.

BANANA STRAWBERRY FLOAT

3/4 cup mashed bananas
3/4 cup mashed strawberries
3/4 cup sugar
Dash of salt

5 cups milk, chilled
1 pint vanilla ice cream
6 whole strawberries

Blend mashed bananas and strawberries with sugar and salt. Add milk and stir to blend. Pour into 6 tall cold glasses and top with ice cream. Garnish with whole strawberries.

Yield: 6 servings

STRAWBERRY COOLER

1 pint fresh strawberries,
    cleaned and sliced
1/3 to 1/2 cup sugar
1/4 cup orange juice

1/2 cup pineapple juice
1 quart milk
1 pint pineapple sherbert

Mash strawberries, stir in sugar. Add orange and pineapple juices; blend in milk. Pour into 4 chilled tall glasses. Top each with a scoop of sherbert. Note: Frozen strawberries may be substituted for fresh ones. Use one 10 ounce package and omit sugar.

Yield: 4 servings.

SPARKLING CRANBERRY PUNCH

1 (32 ounce) bottle cranberry juice cocktail
1 (6-ounce) can frozen orange juice, undiluted
1 (6-ounce) can frozen lemon juice, undiluted
2 cups water
Ice ring or cubes
2 (10-ounce) bottles ginger ale, chilled
Orange slices

Combine fruit juices and water in punch bowl. Just before serving, add ice. Holding bottle on rim of bowl, carefully pour in ginger ale. Garnish with orange slices.   Yield: 18 servings.

LIME DELIGHT

4 cups strong tea, cooled   2 tablespoons sugar
Juice of 1 lime   Lime peel
3 tablespoons maraschino   Cherries
   cherry juice

Combine tea, lime juice, cherry juice, and sugar. Pour over ice cubes in tall glasses. Garnish with a twist of lime peel and a cherry.
                                            Yield 4 to 6 servings.

PLANTER'S PUNCH

1 ounce fresh lime juice   2 ounces light rum or
1 ounce fresh orange juice   red port wine
1 ounce pineaple juice

Fill glass with crushed ice. Pour juices and rum over ice. Serve in tall glass.

Jellies,
Pickles &
Relishes

JELLIES, PICKLES & RELISHES

SAUCES

JELLIES, PICKLES & RELISHES

SWEET CRISP GREEN TOMATO PICKLES

8 pounds green tomatoes
1 (16 ounce) package pickling
  lime
9 cups sugar
3 quarts vinegar

1 tablespoon salt
10 drops green food coloring
  (optional)
2 gallons water

Cut tomatoes into 1/4 inch slices. Mix lime and water well, pour over tomatoes, and let soak for 24 hours. Rinse tomatoes well and soak in cold water for 2 hours. Mix sugar, vinegar, salt, and coloring. Drain tomatoes and add to vinegar-sugar mixture. Soak tomatoes in mixture overnight then bring to boil and let boil for 40 minutes. Pack in clean, hot jars and seal.

Yield: 8 pints

WATERMELON RIND PICKLE

1 quart watermelon cubed
  soaked overnite
4 tablespoons of salt
Water to cover cubes
4 cups sugar
1 whole lime sliced

2 cups vinegar
1 teaspoon mustard seed
1 teaspoon allspice
1 teaspoon ginger
1 teaspoon whole cloves
2 sticks whole cinnamon

Drain watermelon, combine other ingredients. Boil on medium heat until watermelon is clear. Pack in jars and store in refrigerator.

Yield 1/2 gallon

PEAR MINCEMEAT

4 pounds pears
3 pounds sugar
1 pound raisins
1 cup vinegar
1 teaspoon cinnamon

1 teaspoon salt
1 teaspoon cloves
1 teaspoon allspice
1 teaspoon nutmeg

Wash, cut and core pears (do not peel). Grind in chopper with raisins. Add sugar, vinegar, allspice, salt, cinnamon, cloves, and nutmeg. Mix well. Cook until tender. Put in sterilized jars and seal.

OKRA PICKLES

3 1/2 pounds small okra pods
5 cloves garlic
5 small fresh hot peppers
1 quart water

1 pint vinegar
1/3 cup pickling salt
2 teaspoons dillseeds

Pack okra tightly into hot sterilized jars, leaving 1/4 inch headspace.
Place a clove of garlic and a hot pepper in each of the jars.
Combine remaining ingredients in a medium saucepan; bring to a boil.
Pour vinegar mixture over okra, leaving 1/4 inch headspace.
Cover at once with metal lids, and screw bands tight. Process in boiling
water bath 10 minutes. 4 to 5 pints.

SQUASH PICKLES

4 medium-size yellow squash
  sliced 1/4 inch thick
1/2 cup pickling salt
2 small onion, thinly sliced
1/2 cup sugar

1 1/2 cups vinegar
3 tablespoons dry mustard
1 tablespoon ground ginger
1 tablespoon curry powder
6 whole peppercorns

Layer squash and salt in a large glass or plastic container. Cover and let
stand about 4 hours. Rinse squash several times in cold water; Drain
well. Place squash and onion in a large Dutch oven. Combine remaining
ingredients in a small, heavy saucepan, mixing well. Bring to a boil; boil
5 minutes, stirring often.
Pour vinegar mixture over squash: bring mixture to a boil, and cook 5
minutes or just until squash are crisp-tender. Pack into hot sterilized
jars, leaving 1/4 inch headspace.
Cover at once with metal lids, and srew bands tight. Process in boiling
water bath for 15 minutes.

Yield: 2 pints

CORN RELISH

About 18 ears fresh corn
7 quarts water
1 small head cabbage,
  chopped
1 cup chopped onion
1 cup chopped green pepper
1 quart vinegar

1 cup chopped sweet red
  pepper
1 to 2 cups sugar
2 tablespoons dry mustard
1 tablespoon salt
1 tablespoon ground turmeric
1 cup water

Remove husks and silks from corn just before cooking. Bring 7 quarts water to a boil; add corn. Bring water to a second boil; boil 5 minutes. cut corn from cob measuring about 2 quarts of kernels.

Combine corn kernels and remaining ingredients in a large saucepan; simmer over low heat 20 minutes. Bring mixture to a boil. Pack into hot sterilized jars, leaving 1/4 inch headspace.

Cover at once with metal lids, and screw bands tight. Process in boiling water bath for 15 minutes.

Yield: 6 pints

BREAD AND BUTTER PICKLES

1 1/2 gallons sliced tender
  cucumbers
2 medium onions, sliced
1 cup salt
Crushed ice
5 cups sugar

5 cups vinegar
2 teaspoons mustard seed
1 teaspoon celery seed
1 teaspoon ground cloves
2 teaspoons turmeric

Combine cucumbers and onions. Make a layer of cucumber and onion, then layer of salt and ice. Alternate until all is used. Place in refrigerator for 3 hours. Drain and let dry on paper towels.

Mix vinegar, sugar, turmeric, mustard seed, celery seed and cloves. Bring to a full boil and add cucumbers and onions. Do not boil. Just allow to heat through. Stir from the bottom up. Pour into streilize jars and seal.

Yield: 10 to 12 pints

APPLE RELISH

1 gallon apples peeled
    and chopped
8 red sweet pepper
1 quart vinegar
3 cups sugar
2 teaspoon ground turmeric

8 green sweet peppers, ground
5 large onions, ground
2 tablespoons salt
2 teaspoons ground mustard
3 teaspoons ground cinnamon

Combine all ingredients in a large boiler. Bring to a boil and simmer 15 minutes. This recipe can be used for pear relish also.

PEACH BUTTER

1 peck peahces
10 cups sugar
2 whole sticks cinnamon
2 tablespoons cloves
1 tablespoon whole anise

Scald, peel and stone peaches. Cook very slowly, without water, until soft enough to mash to a pulp. Measure about 5 quarts of pulp. Add sugar and spices, and continue to cook very slowly until thick (about 2 hours). Remove spices (which may be tied in bag). Pour into sterilized jars and seal.

TARTAR SAUCE

1/2 teaspoon liquid hot
  pepper sauce
1 teaspoon vinegar
1 cup mayonnaise
1 tablespoon minced onion

1 tablespoon chopped parsley
1 tablespoon chopped green
  olives
2 tablespoons chopped pickles

Stir pepper sauce and vinegar into mayonnaise. Add onion, parsley, olives, and pickles; mix well.

Yield: about 1 1/2 cups

CHILI SAUCE

3 medium onions, chopped
1 bell pepper, chopped
4 to 5 stalks celery, chopped
3 tablespoons oil or grease
1 pound ground meat
1 can tomatoes

1 can tomato soup
1/2 can water
Tabasco sauce
Salt and pepper
Chili powder
Worcestershire sauce

Saute onions, bell pepper, and celery in oil for 2 to 3 minutes. Add meat and cook until meat crumbles. Add tomatoes, soup, water and spices to taste. Cook slowly for one hour. If sauce gets too thick, add more water.

RAISIN SAUCE

1/2 cup brown sugar
1 teaspoon dry mustard
2 tablespoons cornstarch
2 tablespoons vinegar

2 tablespoons lemon juice
1 1/4 cups water
1/4 cup raisins

Mix sugar, mustard, and cornstarch in saucepan. Slowly add vinegar, lemon juice and water. Stir in raisins. Cook over low heat, stirring until thickens.

Yield: 2 cups

INDEX

SALADS

PUDDINGS

SAUCES

LOOK MOM, I CAN COOK

BOARDING HOUSE REACH

Southern cooking at its finest! Recipes from a famous boarding house whose table has become a legend. No gourmet cooking, just old-fashioned terrific food — like eating at grandmother's house!

Washable Plastic Cover   Comb Binder $8.95 Retail

THE COOKBOOK ORGANIZER

A must for every cookbook owner. A "where-to-look book" — no more time wasted searching for a special recipe. Now you can list all those favorites, the page number & cookbook where they can be found.

Washable Plastic Cover   Comb Binder $5.95 Retail

HELP! COMPANY'S COMING

great book for brides, bachelors, and busy people. More than just a cookbook — it's a quick course in uying, storing and tastefully cooking. Old fashioned favorites from simple, easy-to-follow recipes.

Hard Cover   Comb Binder $10.95 Retail

GOLDEN ISLES CUISINE

beautiful book from Coastal Georgia. Terrific recipes. Its 14 sections include everything from superb eafood to Elmer Fudpucker Cake.

Hard Cover   Comb Binder $9.95 Retail

THE BACHELOR'S COOKBOOK

great book for the working bachelors, college students, married guys sharing K.P. duty and bachelorettes. imple but good food, with easy to follow, step by step directions. Recipes men can understand, prepare and eally enjoy eating.

Washable Plastic Cover   Comb Binder $6.95 Retail

LOOK MOM, I CAN COOK!

Children of all ages will enjoy this book. Easy-to-read recipes for food as well as "Extra Fun In The Kitchen" ection.

Washable Plastic Cover   Comb Binder $6.95 Retail

end Orders To:
ot Gibson Publications ● P.O. Box 117, Waycross, Ga. 31502
dd $1.25 postage & handling for first book — 50¢ for each additional book.

- -

end To: _____

treet: _____

City: _____ State: _____ Zip: _____

Quan.	Book Title	Price

Check Or Money Order	Total	
Enclosed for _____	P&H	
	Ga. Sales Tax	
	Total	

Names and addresses of bookstores, gift shops, etc.
in your area would be appreciated.

_____

_____

_____

_____

_____

_____

_____